GOD'S WRIT IN THE QUR'AN

GOD'S WRIT IN THE QUR'AN

A GUIDANCE FOR THE GOD-FEARING

SAID MIRZA

Men of God Publishing | willyounotreason.com

Copyright © 2024 by Said Mirza
All rights reserved. This book or any portion thereof
may not be reproduced or used in any manner whatsoever
without the express written permission of the publisher
except for the use of brief quotations.

First Edition, 2024

ISBN 978-1-7336408-6-2
The Qur'an: A Complete Revelation © Sam Gerrans, 2021.
Cover image by Marie-Lan Nguyen 'Folio from the "Blue Qur'an"
(MET 2004.88)' licensed under Creative Commons Attribution 2.5
https://creativecommons.org/licenses/by/2.5/

This book can be downloaded for free at:
willyounotreason.com

God's Writ:
A written set of commands from God to mankind

"Is it other than God I should seek as judge when He it is that sent down to you the Writ set out and detailed?" And those to whom We gave the Writ know that it is sent down from thy Lord with the truth; so be thou not of those who doubt.

And perfected is the word of thy Lord in truth and justice; there is none to change His words; and He is the Hearing, the Knowing.

(The Qur'an 6:114-115)

CONTENTS

Introduction	ix
Chapter 1: God's Writ	1
Chapter 2: Marriage	13
Chapter 3: Divorce	19
Chapter 4: Inheritance	28
Chapter 5: Food	34
Chapter 6: Fatherless	42
Chapter 7: Commerce	48
Chapter 8: Retaliation	53
Chapter 9: Charity	65
Chapter 10: Sexual Immorality	76
Chapter 11: Modesty	81
Chapter 12: Parting Words	88
Other Works by the Author	91
Reference	101

INTRODUCTION

All praise be to God for guiding me to the truth and granting me the resources for the commission of this work. Our Lord: take us not to task if we forget or err. Excuse us, forgive us and have mercy upon us; You are our Protector. Help us against the deniers.

> *alif lām mīm*
> **That is the Writ** about which there is no doubt, **a guidance to those of prudent fear:**
> Those who believe in the Unseen, **and uphold the duty,** and of what We have provided them they spend;
> And those who believe in what was sent down to thee, and what was sent down before thee, and of the Hereafter they are certain:
> **Those are upon guidance from their Lord; and it is they who are the successful.**
> (The Qur'an 2:1-5)

The Qur'an, God's final revelation, contains within it God's Writ: a written set of commands from God to mankind. It is the *duty* of each and every believer to follow the Writ of God *exclusively*. The importance of this imperative cannot be overstated; God assures success to those who follow His Writ in this life and the hereafter.

In this work, I have organized (and where necessary, explained) God's various commands in His Writ as they relate to specific matters such as marriage, divorce, inheritance, commerce etc. I believe this work will be of benefit to a sincere believer who has made the decision to implement the Writ of God in his personal and communal life.[1] This book is not an exhaustive compilation of all the commands present in God's Writ; God willing that will be done later.

I wish to thank Brother Gerrans for allowing me to use his translation in this work. When reading the footnotes please be aware that I have (where necessary) added Brother Gerrans' helpful commentary in addition to mine. His thoughts are prefixed with *SG*. My thoughts are prefixed with *SM*.

Brother Gerrans' full translation of the Qur'an (The Qur'an: A Complete Revelation) and his accompanying commentary is available for free here: https://reader.quranite.com

---

[1] SM: As a man I am entirely fallible and you should not follow my interpretation blindly. It is the responsibility of each and every believer to verify the information presented here and study the Qur'an carefully; every man is accountable for his actions on the Day of Judgment: "That no bearer of burdens bears the burden of another," (53:38)

1
GOD'S WRIT

> God it is who has sent down the Writ with the truth and the balance. And what can make thee know that the Hour might be nigh!
> (42:17)

Most translators of the Qur'an, in accordance with its ordinary usage, translate the word *al-kitab* as *the Book*.[2] However, the Qur'an uses this word to mean something specific; a pan-textual analysis[3] of *al-kitab* reveals it to mean *the Writ*[4] i.e. a written set of commands from God to mankind. In other words, what God means by the word *al-kitab* is His written commands which He has mandated be followed and not simply *the Book*.

The Writ vs the Book

Consider the following verses in which the translation of *al-kitab* as *the Writ* fits perfectly and gives a better understanding of the verse (as opposed to a generic translation of *the Book*).

---

2 SM: See translations by Arberry, Yusuf Ali, & Saheeh International of verse 2:2 where *al-kitab* occurs for the first time in the Qur'an.
3 SM: Looking at the usage of a word or phrase across the entire text of the Qur'an to derive its meaning.
4 SM: I am indebted to Brother Gerrans for this insight and direct the interested reader to his study of this term in "The Addenda to the Qur'an: A Complete Revelation (Page 24)": https://quranite.com/wp-content/uploads/Addenda-to-The-Quran-A-Complete-Revelation.pdf

> Then are you those who kill your own, and turn a faction among you out of their homes, assisting one another against them in sin and enmity; and if they come to you as captives, you ransom them, **but unlawful for you was their expulsion. Do you believe in part of the Writ[5] and deny part?** Then what is the reward of him among you who does that save disgrace in the life of this world? And on the Day of Resurrection they are sent back to the harshest punishment; and God is not unmindful of what you do.
> (2:85)

In the above verse, God is chiding the children of Israel for denying (not implementing) part of the *al-kitab* which they possess i.e. they are in violation of one of His commands present in the Writ given to them: *to not expel one of their own.*

> Mankind was one community; **then God raised up prophets as bearers of glad tidings and warners, and sent down with them the Writ[6] with the truth, that He might judge between men concerning that wherein they differed.** And there differed therein only those who were given it, after clear signs had come to them, through sectarian zealotry between them. But God guided those who heeded warning to that of the truth concerning which they differed, by His leave; and God guides whom He wills to a straight path.
> (2:213)

In the above verse, God says that He sent down with the prophets "the Writ with the truth, that He might judge between men concerning that wherein they differed." This judgment will be on the Day of Judgment (when all men will be resurrected).[7] Therefore, what is meant here is that God has sent down the Writ (a written set of commands)

5 SM: Arabic: *al-kitab*.
6 SM: Arabic: *al-kitab*.
7 SM: See 2:113, 2:213, 3:55, 10:19, 10:93, 16:124, 22:69, 32:25, 39:3, 39:46, 43:63, 45:17 for support of this explanation.

and mankind will be judged on the Day of Judgment on the basis of this Writ.

> And they measured God not with the measure due Him. And the earth altogether will be His handful on the Day of Resurrection, and the heavens will be folded up in His right hand. Glory be to Him! And exalted is He above that to which they ascribe a partnership!
> And the Trumpet will be blown, and whoso is in the heavens and whoso is in the earth will fall down thunderstruck save whom God wills. **Then will it be blown again; and then will they be standing, looking on.**
> And the earth will shine with the light of its Lord; **and the Writ will be set up, and the prophets and the witnesses will be brought,** and it will be concluded between them with justice, and they will not be wronged.
> And every soul will be paid in full for what it did; and He best knows what they do.
> (39:67-70)

The above verse confirms our understanding: God will judge mankind on the Day of Judgment on the basis of His Writ; the same Writ which he has sent down to His prophets throughout the ages. Imagine the state of those who were unaware of the existence of God's Writ—let alone that they had to follow it! I hope this shows you how critical understanding and following God's Writ really is.

> Hast thou not considered those given a portion of the Writ?[8] **They are invited to the Writ[9] of God, that it might judge between them,** then a faction of them turns away; and they are averse,
> (3:23)

---

8 SM: Arabic: *al-kitab*.
9 SM: Arabic: *kitab*.

> **We have sent down to thee the Writ**[10] **with the truth, that thou mightest judge between men by what God has shown thee;** and be thou not an advocate for the treacherous;
> (4:105)

The above two verses make it clear that the function of the *Writ* is to enable the prophet (and by extension, the believers) to judge between men. In other words, the prophet (and messenger) Muhammad was commanded to judge between men using God's Writ present in the Qur'an (which was revealed to him). The significance of this will be discussed later.

Why is this important?

You might be wondering what the point of the above discussion is? Why does it matter if *al-kitab* means *the Writ* instead of *the Book*? It is important because if we understand *al-kitab* to simply mean *the Book*, we lose sight of the point of the *al-kitab*; that it represents God's commands to mankind. Our entire success (in this life and the hereafter) hinges on following God's commands in His Writ. Consider the opening verses of the second chapter of the Qur'an:

> *alif lām mīm*
> **That is the Writ about which there is no doubt, a guidance to those of prudent fear:**
> Those who believe in the Unseen, and uphold the duty, and of what We have provided them they spend;
> And those who believe in what was sent down to thee, and what was sent down before thee, and of the Hereafter they are certain:
> **Those are upon guidance from their Lord; and it is they who are the successful.**
> (2:1-5)

God makes it clear that the Writ *is* guidance and that those who

---
10 SM: Arabic: *al-kitab*.

follow this guidance will be *the successful*. Muslims have abandoned God's Writ in favor of the *Sharia Law*. God has not let this perfidiousness of Muslims gone unpunished[11] as is evident by their sad state of affairs today.[12]

Sharia Law

The *Sharia* Law in the religion of Islam is a collection of laws derived from both the Qur'an and the *hadith* (alleged sayings and actions of the prophet and messenger Muhammad) i.e. Muslims use two sources to derive their *Sharia* Law. However, the Qur'an claims to be clear, complete and detailed[13] and, therefore, as believers, we must take *only* the Writ contained (and preserved) in the Qur'an as a source of Law.

It is by means of the *hadith* literature that the scholars of Islam add to, abrogate or modify God's clear commands (His Writ) present in the Qur'an. For example, God is explicit that the children of the deceased must be given their God-ordained shares of the inheritance *before* any other disbursement of funds.[14] Yet, the *Sharia* Law has a whole host of parties who must be paid before the children can get their shares. The *Sharia* Law also forbids certain persons from getting their God-ordained shares when no such stipulations exist in the Writ of God.[15]

If we seriously believe in the Qur'an's claim to be clear, complete and detailed then it follows that we should look to it *exclusively* for guidance on matters which are within the scope of God's Writ. That is to say, we should follow God's Writ exclusively in regards to the subjects it touches

---
11 SM: "...And whoso judges not by what God has sent down: it is they who are the wrongdoers." (5:45)

12 SM: I am here definitely not asserting that the Western (secular) civilization is any better. Both the secularists and religionists are doomed as they have abandoned God's commands in favor of men's.

13 SM: See 2:185, 2:208-209, 4:174, 5:15-16, 5:48-50, 6:105, 6:112-116, 7:52, 10:15, 12:1-2, 12:102-111, 14:52, 15:1, 16:89, 17:9-12, 17:82, 17:41, 17:105-106, 18:54, 24:1, 25:25-33, 26:192-195, 27:76-79, 27:91-92, 28:85-88, 30:58, 31:27, 34:43, 36:69-70, 39:27-28, 41:1-4, 43:1-5, 55:1-4, 75:16-19, 57:9, 85:21-22 for support of using the terms *clear*, *complete* and *detailed*.

14 SM: See Chapter 4.

15 SM: See "The book pertaining to the rules of inheritance": https://www.iium.edu.my/deed/hadith/muslim/011_smt.html

upon (marriage, divorce, inheritance, etc). We cannot add to, abrogate or modify the clear commands present in God's Writ.

However, we see no impediment in creating, following and improving upon laws in regards to subjects which are not within the scope of God's Writ as long as they do not encroach upon (or conflict) with God's Writ.

The doctrine of the believers

> **The doctrine with God is submission.** And those given the Writ differed only after knowledge had come to them, through sectarian zealotry between them; and whoso denies the proofs of God — then is God swift in reckoning.
> (3:19)

> Say thou: "O mankind: **if you are in doubt about my doctrine: I serve not those whom you serve besides God; but I serve God,** who will take you; and I am commanded to be of the believers;
> (10:104)

The doctrine of the believers is submission to God alone which entails *submission to His Writ alone*. It is vital that we allow only what God has allowed and forbid only what God has forbidden *in His Writ*; nothing more, nothing less. As believers it our duty to defy any law which allows what God has forbidden and forbids what God has allowed.[16]

> The revelation of the Writ is from God, the Exalted in Might, the Wise.
> **We sent down to thee the Writ with the truth; so serve thou God, sincere to Him in doctrine.**
> Does not the sincere doctrine belong to God? And those who take allies besides Him: — "We only serve them that they might bring us near to God in proximity!" — God

---

[16] Present day governments and religions prove their open rebellion to God and His Writ by routinely allowing what God has forbidden and forbidding what God has allowed.

will judge between them concerning that wherein they differ; God guides not him who is a liar and an ingrate.
(39:1-3)

Forbidden to you is carrion, and blood, and the flesh of swine, and that dedicated to other than God, and the strangled, and the beaten, and the fallen, and the gored, and that eaten by the beast of prey save what you slaughter, and that sacrificed upon the altar, and that you seek apportionment by divining arrows — that is perfidy — **(this day have those who ignore warning despaired of your doctrine,** so fear them not, but fear Me; **this day have I perfected for you your doctrine** and completed My favour upon you, **and approved for you submission as doctrine)** but whoso is compelled by hunger, without inclination to sin — God is forgiving and merciful.
(5:3)

If they have partners which ordained for them of doctrine that for which God has not given leave[...]. And had it not been for the word of decision, it would have been concluded between them; and the wrongdoers have a painful punishment.
(42:21)

He ordained for you of doctrine what He enjoined upon Noah, and that We have revealed to thee, and what We enjoined upon Abraham and Moses and Jesus: **"Uphold the doctrine, and be not divided therein."** Difficult for the idolaters is that to which thou invitest them. God chooses for Himself whom He wills, and guides to Himself him who turns in repentance.
And they became divided only after knowledge came to them, through sectarian zealotry between them. And were it not for a word that preceded from thy Lord to a stated term, it would have been concluded between

them. And those who were caused to inherit the Writ after them are in sceptical doubt concerning it.

So to that[17] then call thou. And keep thou to the path as thou art commanded, and follow thou not their vain desires, **but say thou: "I believe[18] in what God sent down of Writ, and I have been commanded to be just among you.** God is our Lord and your Lord. We have our works, and you have your works; there is no argument between us and you; God will bring us together, and to Him is the journey's end."

And those who dispute concerning God after that answer has been made to him: their argument has no weight with their Lord; and upon them is wrath, and they have a severe punishment.

God it is who has sent down the Writ with the truth and the balance. And what can make thee know that the Hour might be nigh!

(42:13-17)

All prophets were commanded to judge by God's Writ

All prophets were commanded to judge using the Writ of God entrusted to them. They had no authority to add to, abrogate or modify God's commands in His Writ. Similarly, the prophet Muhammad was commanded to judge men using God's Writ present in the Qur'an. The implication is that even if the *hadith* literature are the actual sayings and actions of Muhammad, they cannot be used as a source of Law; only God's Writ can be used as *the* source of Law.

And how come they to thee for judgment when they have the Torah wherein is the judgment of God, then turn away after that? **And those are not believers. We sent down the Torah wherein is guidance and light. The prophets who submitted judged thereby**

---
17 SM: To God's doctrine.
18 SM: To *believe in the Writ* is not to simply claim to believe in it but to implement the commands present in it. See 2:85.

those who hold to Judaism as did the rabbis and the religious scholars with what they were given charge of the Writ of God and were thereto witnesses: "So fear not mankind but fear Me; and sell not My proofs at a cheap price." **And whoso judges not by what God has sent down, it is they who are the false claimers of guidance.**

And We prescribed for them therein a life for a life, and an eye for an eye, and a nose for a nose, and an ear for an ear, and a tooth for a tooth, and for wounds just requital; but whoso forgives it by way of charity, it is an expiation for him. **And whoso judges not by what God has sent down: it is they who are the wrongdoers.**

And We sent Jesus, son of Mary in their footsteps confirming what was before him of the Torah; and We gave him the Gospel wherein was guidance and light, both confirming what was before him of the Torah and as guidance and admonition for those of prudent fear.

And let the people of the Gospel judge by what God sent down therein; **and whoso judges not by what God has sent down: it is they who are the perfidious.**

(5:43-47)

Muhammad did not issue rulings

And they ask thee for a ruling concerning women. Say thou: "God gives you the ruling concerning them," — and what is recited to you in the Writ concerning the fatherless women (to whom you give not what is prescribed for them, and yet desire to marry them) and concerning the oppressed among children; and that you stand up for equity for the fatherless. And whatever you do of good, God knows it.

(4:127)

They ask thee for a ruling. Say thou: "God gives you the ruling concerning those without an immediate

heir: if a man perishes without a child but has a sister: for her is half of what he left, and he inherits from her if she has not a child. But if there are two females: for them is two-thirds of what he left. And if they are brethren, men and women: for the male is the like of the share of two females." And God makes plain to you lest you go astray; and God knows all things.
(4:176)

The above verses should suffice to show that the prophet and messenger Muhammad could not issue any laws; God issues laws. God's Writ preserved in the Qur'an contains within it all that is needed to judge between men.

Muhammad was commanded to judge by God's Writ

We have sent down to thee the Writ[19] with the truth, that thou mightest judge between men by what God has shown thee; and be thou not an advocate for the treacherous;
(4:105)

And We sent down to thee the Writ[20] with the truth, confirming what is before it of the Writ,[21] [22] and as a control over it. **So judge thou between them by what God has sent down;** and follow thou not their vain desires away from what has come to thee of the truth. For each of you We appointed an ordinance and a procedure. And had God willed, He could have made you one community; but that He might try you in what He gave you[...]. — So vie in good deeds; unto God will you return all together, and He will inform you of that wherein you differed — **And judge thou between them by what God has sent down;** and follow thou not their vain desires, and beware

---
19 SM: Arabic: *al-kitab*.
20 SM: Arabic: *al-kitab*.
21 SM: Arabic: *al-kitab*.
22 SM: i.e. confirming the Writ given to Moses before.

thou of them lest they seduce thee away from some of what God has sent down to thee. And if they turn away, know thou that God but intends to afflict them for some of their transgressions; and many among men are perfidious.

Is it the judgment of ignorance they seek? And who is better than God in judgment for people who are certain? (5:48-50)

We have sent down manifest proofs; and God guides whom He wills to a straight path.

And they say: "We believe in God and the Messenger, and we obey"; then a faction among them turns away after that — and those are not believers.

And when they are invited to God and His messenger, that he judge between them,[23] then a faction among them turns away.

But if the truth be theirs, they come to him in willing submission.

Is there in their hearts a disease? If they doubt, or fear that God would deal unjustly with them — or would His messenger: — nay, it is they who are the wrongdoers.

The only word of the believers, when they are invited to God and His messenger, that he judge between them, is that they say: "We hear and we obey," — and it is they who are the successful.

And whoso obeys God and His messenger, and fears God, and is in prudent fear of Him: — it is they who are the attainers of success.

(24:46-52)

The prophet and messenger Muhammad was commanded to "judge thou between them by what God has sent down".[24] When a faction of

---

23 SM: Using the manifest proofs God has sent down to him i.e. God's Writ (See 24:46, 5:48-50).

24 SM: "And judge thou between them by what God has sent down; and follow thou not their vain desires, and beware thou of them lest they seduce thee away from some of what God has sent down to thee. And if they turn away, know thou that God but intends to

those who claimed that they believed in God and His messenger was "invited to God and His messenger, that he judge between them,"[25] they turned away because they did not want to be judged by what God had sent down i.e. His Writ.

Similarly, Muslims of today (who claim to obey God and His messenger), when invited to be judged by God's Writ, turn away preferring instead to go to their *muftis* (who use sources in addition to God's Writ) or secular judges (who judge using man-made laws) for judgment. Those who turn away from the judgment of God are the wrongdoers.[26]

Are we to seek a judge other than God?

> **"Is it other than God I should seek as judge when He it is that sent down to you the Writ set out and detailed?"** And those to whom We gave the Writ know that it is sent down from thy Lord with the truth; so be thou not of those who doubt.
> And perfected is the word of thy Lord in truth and justice; there is none to change His words; and He is the Hearing, the Knowing.
> (6:114-115)

God requires us to judge using His Writ alone. We must strive to understand and implement God's Writ exclusively which God has preserved in the Qur'an.

We shall now proceed with the task of collating and considering the various commands of God as they relate to the subjects of marriage, food, commerce etc. You will see that not only is God's Writ practical and simple to understand but also allows for a great deal of flexibility in its implementation. You will also notice that God's Writ is complete i.e. it provides complete instructions on a particular subject.

---

afflict them for some of their transgressions; and many among men are perfidious." (5:49)
25 SM: "And when they are invited to God and His messenger, that he judge between them, then a faction among them turns away." (24:48)
26 SM: See 24:50.

2
MARRIAGE

And among His proofs is that He created for you spouses from yourselves that you might be reassured thereby, and made between you love and mercy; in that are proofs for people who reflect.
(30:21)

Allowed and forbidden marriage candidates

And marry not idolatresses[27] until they believe. And a believing[28] slave girl is better than an idolatress, though she impress you. And give not in marriage to idolaters until they believe. And a believing slave is better than an idolater, though he impress you. Those invite to the Fire; and God invites to the Garden and forgiveness, by His leave. And He makes plain His proofs to men, that they might take heed.
(2:221)

---

27 SM: See the following list of verses to see who an *idolater* is: 3:64, 5:72, 6:19, 6:75-79, 7:189-191, 9:31, 10:18, 14:22, 16:86, 18:32-44, 40:12.

28 SM: This is a good summary of a believing woman: "O Prophet: when the believing women come to thee, swearing fealty to thee: — that they will not ascribe a partnership with God to anything; and they will not steal; and they will not commit unlawful sexual intercourse; and they will not kill their children; and they will not produce a calumny they have invented between their hands and their feet; and they will not disobey thee in what is fitting; — then accept thou their fealty, and ask thou God to forgive them; God is forgiving and merciful." (60:12)

The unchaste[29] man shall not marry save an unchaste woman or an idolatress; and an unchaste woman shall not marry save an unchaste man or an idolater — and that is unlawful to the believers —
(24:3)

And give in marriage the unmarried[30] among you, and the righteous among your male slaves and your female slaves; if they be poor, God will enrich them out of His bounty; and God is encompassing and knowing.
And let abstain those who find not[31] marriage until God enriches them out of His bounty. And those who seek the writ from among those your right hands possess:[32] contract with them if you know good to be in them; and give to them out of the wealth God has given you. And compel not your slave-girls to whoredom, if they desire chastity[...] — seeking the enjoyment of the life of this world. And whoso compels them, then God, after their compulsion, is forgiving and merciful.
(24:32-33)

And marry not what your fathers married[33] among women save what is past; it was sexual immorality, and hateful, and an evil path.
Forbidden to you are your mothers, and your daughters, and your sisters, and your paternal aunts, and your maternal aunts, and the daughters of your brother, and the daughters of your sister, and your milk-mothers, and

---

29 SG: The root (z-n-y) conveys senses of *unlawful sexual intercourse* (sexual congress between two people who are not married to each other) and occurs at 17:32, 24:2, 24:2, 24:3, 24:3, 24:3, 24:3, 25:68, 60:12.
30 SM: Arberry translates as *spouseless*. Lane's lexicon states: "She had no husband; said of a virgin and of one who is not a virgin".
31 SG: i.e. find not the means for.
32 SM: We will ignore directives for what a believer's *right hands possess* (commonly termed as slaves) since such a class is not legally recognized anymore.
33 SG: I take this to close the door to two sins at once: the sin of sexual relations with a previous wife of one's father, and any attempt to increase one's share of one's father's estate by marrying his widow.

your milk-sisters, and the mothers of your wives, and your step-daughters under your protection from your wives unto whom you have gone in (and if you have gone not in unto them, then there is no wrong upon you) and the wives of your sons of your loins, and that you bring two sisters together, save what is past; God is forgiving and merciful;

And ~~married~~ *chaste*[34] women[35] save what your right hands possess.[36] The Writ of God is over you. But lawful to you is what is beyond that, if you seek with your wealth in chastity, not being fornicators. And what you enjoy thereby of them: give them their rewards as an obligation.[37] And there is no wrong upon you in what you do by mutual agreement after the obligation; God is knowing and wise.

And whoso among you has not the means to marry ~~free~~[38] chaste[39] believing women, then from what your right hands possess of believing maids; and God best knows your faith. You are of one another, so marry them with the leave of their people; and give them their rewards according to what is fitting, they being chaste and not fornicators, nor taking secret friends. But when they are in wedlock, then if they commit sexual immorality: upon them is half what is due the ~~free~~ chaste[40] women of punishment; that is for him who fears hardship among

---

34 SM: I have replaced *married* with *chaste*; this is the pan-textual meaning after we analyze all instances of it in 4:24, 4:25, 5:5, 24:4 and 24:23.

35 SM: i.e. chaste women of the common-folk. See discussion *We cannot marry chaste women of the women-folk* below.

36 SM: See discussion under *We cannot marry chaste women of the common-folk* below.

37 SM: A man must pay an amount to the woman.

38 SG: Arabic: *muḥṣināt* — chaste (women). The apposition is between chaste (i.e. someone known to have had sexual relations only within marriage) and someone about whom that is not known; *muḥṣināt* are women protected — from within the culture or tribe — not those brought in as captives (by war or purchase) whose past is not known. The word *muḥṣināt* is often translated as free in such contexts (which I have done here) which is correct in principle but requires additional information to be understood.

39 SM: See note to 4:24.

40 SM: See note to 4:24.

you. And that you be patient is best for you; and God is
forgiving and merciful.
(4:22-25)

We cannot marry chaste women of the common-folk

While Brother Gerrans has translated *muhsanatu* as *married women* in verse 4:24, I have opted to use *chaste* to keep its meaning consistently in line with its usage throughout the Qur'an.[41] Verse 24:3 forbids *unchaste women* to the believers and verse 4:24 also forbids *chaste women of the common folk*[42] to the believers, effectively leaving only *chaste believing women* or *chaste women of those given the Writ before* as possible candidates[43] for a believing man. The below verse confirms this understanding.

> This day are good things made lawful for you; and the food of those given the Writ is lawful for you, and your food is lawful for them, as are chaste women among the believing women and chaste women among those given the Writ before you, when you have given them their dowries,[44] being chaste and not fornicators, nor taking secret friends. And whoso denies the faith: his work has been in vain, and he in the Hereafter is among the losers.
> (5:5)

Marriage procedure

> O you who heed warning: when the believing women come to you as émigrées: examine them. God best knows their faith. And if you know them to be believing women, then return them not to the atheists. Such women are not lawful for them, and they are not lawful for such

---

[41] SM: A complete list of occurrences of this word: 4:24, 4:25, 5:5, 24:4, 24:23.
[42] SM: Common-folk: Those who are not given the Writ or are not implementing it.
[43] SM: We will not look at the exception to marrying chaste women of the common- folk in the case of what a believer's *right hands possess* (commonly termed as slaves) since this class of people are is not legally recognized anymore.
[44] SM: Lit: *rewards*; A man must pay an amount to a woman.

women. And give them[45] what they spent. And you do no wrong to marry such women when you give them their rewards.[46] And hold not by tie denying women; and ask for what you have spent,[47] and let them[48] ask for what they have spent. That is the judgment of God; He judges between you; and God is knowing and wise.
And if any of your wives slip away from you to the atheists, then you are met with the same:[49] give those whose wives have gone the like of what they spent; and be in prudent fear of God in whom you are believers. (60:10-11)

Marrying a believing widow

And those of you who die and leave behind wives: they[50] shall wait by themselves four months and ten.[51] And when they[52] have reached their term, then you do no wrong in what they[53] do concerning themselves according to what is fitting. And God is aware of what you do.
And you do no wrong in what you intimate to women of proposal, or hide within yourselves; God knows that you will remember them.[54] But make not nor take an oath with them[55] secretly save that you speak a fitting word. And do not decide upon the knot of marriage until the writ reaches its term.[56] And know that God knows what

---

45 SG: i.e. the atheists. Grammar: masculine plural object pronoun.
46 SM: A man must pay an amount to the woman.
47 SM: Ask for your payment to be returned.
48 SG: i.e. the atheists.
49 SM: Arberry renders as *retaliate*. I take this to mean that if a disbelieving woman goes over from the believers to the unbelievers and a believing woman comes over from the unbelievers to the believers, the believer must still pay her unbelieving husband the amount he spent.
50 SG: Grammar: feminine plural.
51 SG: i.e. four lunar months and ten days.
52 SG: Grammar: feminine plural.
53 SG: Grammar: feminine plural.
54 SG: Grammar: feminine plural.
55 SG: Grammar: feminine plural.
56 SM: four lunar months and ten days have passed as per 2:234.

is within your souls, so fear Him. And know that God is forgiving and clement.
(2:234-235)

Taking of oaths

Although the above verses are in the context of marrying women whose husbands have died, a close reading of 2:235 makes it clear that an oath must be taken as part of the due process of marriage. This is also referred to obliquely in 4:21.[57]

In conclusion, a believing man can only marry a believing woman or a woman from the people of the Writ (communities that implement God's Writ). The mechanics of getting married are straight-forward; they involve the man giving the woman a payment, and the taking of oaths.

We shall now look at the procedure for divorce in the Writ of God.

---

57 SM: "And how can you take it after you have gone in unto each other, and they have taken from you a solemn agreement?" (4:21)

3
DIVORCE

> And if they decide on divorce, then God is hearing and knowing.
> (2:227)

To start out, the Qur'an outlines the proper roles and responsibilities of a husband and wife. By holding on to these God-ordained rules, a couple has a fighting chance to create and maintain a healthy marriage.

> Men are responsible for women by what God has favoured one of them over another, and by what they spend of their wealth; and the righteous women are humbly obedient, keeping unseen what God keeps.[58] And those from whom you fear contempt: admonish them; and leave them in beds apart; and strike them. But if they obey you, then seek not a path against them; God is exalted and great.
> And if you[59] fear a breach between them, raise up an arbitrator from his family and an arbitrator from her family. If they desire right ordering, God will reconcile them; God is knowing and aware.
> (4:34-35)

The take-away from the above is that a believer must try to work

---
58 SM: The proper roles and responsibilities of husband and wife are outlined.
59 SG: This references the wider community of believers.

things out with his wife before initiating divorce. However, if the divorce is initiated, then the Writ is clear: a husband cannot take back what he has given to a wife unless she has committed manifest sexual immorality[60] or that she herself gives it over to facilitate an easy exit from the marriage.[61]

> O you who heed warning: it is not lawful for you to inherit from women against their will;[62] and neither constrain them that you might take away part of what you gave them save that they commit manifest sexual immorality.[63] And live with them according to what is fitting. And if you dislike them, it may be that you dislike a thing and God makes therein much good.
> And if you wish to replace one wife with another[64] and you have given one of them a fortune, take not from it anything; would you take it through false accusation and obvious sin?[65]
> And how can you take it after you have gone in unto each other, and they have taken from you a solemn agreement? (4:19-21)

Divorce process

---

60 SM: See Chapter 10 to see what actions constitute it.
61 SM: See 2:229.
62 SG: Lit.: *forcibly*. The Traditionalist generally, somewhat predictably — and incorrectly — reads this to mean that one may not inherit the woman herself. The plain purport of the verse in a context (prior to a related aside which then feeds back into the main subject) of right financial dealings with women is: *you may not compel a wife to leave you her substance when she dies by retaining her purely to inherit from her on her death or by disallowing her right to make bequests*. In Qur'anic usage *waratha* + direct object (as here) means to *inherit from* (see an example at 4:11) and *not to inherit* (e.g. *something*). Though I was unaware of Muhammad Asad's thought on this subject at the time of my analysis, I include part of this comment here for broader context: According to one of the interpretations advanced by Zamakhshari, *this refers to a man's forcibly keeping an unloved wife - and thus preventing her from marrying another man - in the hope of inheriting her property under the provisions specified in the first sentence of verse 12 above.*
63 SM: See Chapter 10 to see actions that constitute it.
64 SM: This flies in the face of the Muslim practice of taking up to 4 wives. See Chapter 6 for an in-depth discussion on polygamy within the Writ of God.
65 SM: i.e. by falsely accusing one's wife of sexual immorality to take back what is rightfully hers.

Divorce is a two-part process; a cooling-off period in which the woman must wait four lunar months after her husband renounces his marriage-oath. The husband can return to her if he so wishes (i.e. changes his mind).

After the cooling-off period, divorce proceedings can resume, if the husband so wishes. His wife must wait by herself (i.e. not have any sexual relations) for three menstrual courses (to confirm she is not pregnant). If she is not menstruating, she needs to wait three lunar months. In either case, at any time the husband can take her back.

If she is not pregnant, then the husband either has to take her back or release her after this period. If she is pregnant, then the husband either has to take her back or release her after she gives birth (i.e. a pregnant woman cannot be divorced).

If the couple do not come to a reconciliation and the waiting period has elapsed, the divorce is final and must be witnessed by two just men among the believers.

> And make not God a cover for your oaths, to keep you from virtue and prudent fear and making right between men. And God is hearing and knowing.
> God will not take you to task for the vain speech in your oaths, but He will take you to task for what your hearts earned. And God is forgiving and clement.
> For those who forswear their women is a wait of four months;[66] but if they return,[67] then God is forgiving and merciful.
> And if they decide on divorce, then God is hearing and knowing.
> And divorced women shall wait by themselves[68] three menstrual courses; and it is not lawful for them to

---

66 SG: Arabic: *shahr* — moon, month. My personal opinion is that in all cases where months are the measure of waiting it means a period beginning at the next new moon, the reason is that this method provides the most transparency for the community. See also note to 2:189.
67 SG: i.e. if they change their minds, and go back to their women.
68 SM: They are not to engage in further sexual relations otherwise there is no point in

conceal what God has created in their wombs, if they believe in God and the Last Day. And their husbands are worthier[69] to take them back during that[70] if they desire right ordering. And due to women is the like of what is due from them, according to what is fitting, but men have a degree over them.[71] And God is exalted in might and wise.

Divorce is twice. Then retaining according to what is fitting, or releasing with good conduct. And it is not lawful for you to take of what you have given women unless they fear that they cannot uphold the limits of God. Then if you[72] fear that they cannot uphold the limits of God, they do no wrong concerning that whereby she ransoms herself.[73] Those are the limits of God, so transgress them not. And whoso transgresses the limits of God, it is they who are the wrongdoers.

And if he has divorced her, she is not lawful to him thereafter until she marries a spouse other than him. Then if he[74] divorces her, they do no wrong to return to each other, if they think that they can uphold the limits of God. And those are the limits of God; He makes them plain for people who know.

And when you divorce women, and they have reached their term, then retain them according to what is fitting or release them according to what is fitting. And retain them not through harm, to transgress; and whoso does that has wronged himself. And take not the proofs of God in mockery; and remember the favour of God upon you, and what He has sent down to you of the Writ and

---

stipulating the wait period of three menstrual cycles in 2:228.
69 SM: i.e. have more right.
70 SG: i.e. over the period just mentioned.
71 SG: The context is clear: responsibility for initiative falls to the man.
72 SG: A careful reading indicates the involvement of an outside party made up of believers.
73 SG: i.e. the man has no claim over that which he has given the woman. However, the woman can choose to return what she likes to him if she wishes in order to facilitate an exit from the marriage.
74 SG: i.e. the second husband.

wisdom whereby He admonishes you. And be in prudent fear of God, and know that God knows all things.

And when you divorce women, and they have reached their term, then constrain them not from marrying their spouses when they have come to terms according to what is fitting. By that is admonished whoso among you believes in God and the Last Day; that is purer and cleaner for you; and God knows, and you know not.

And mothers shall suckle their children two complete years, for such as wish to complete the suckling. And upon the father is their[75] provision and their[76] clothing, according to what is fitting. No soul is burdened save to its capacity. A mother shall not be hurt by her child, nor a father by his child. And upon the heir is the like of that. And if they[77] desire weaning by mutual consent and consultation between them,[78] then they[79] do no wrong. And if you desire to seek one to suckle your children, then you do no wrong when you deliver what you have brought according to what is fitting. And be in prudent fear of God, and know that God sees what you do. (2:224-233)

Dissolution of marriage in case of death of husband

And those of you who die and leave behind wives: they shall wait by themselves four months and ten.[80] And when they have reached their term, then you do no wrong in what they do concerning themselves according to what is fitting. And God is aware of what you do. And you do no wrong in what you intimate to women of proposal, or hide within yourselves; God knows that you will remember them. But make not nor take an oath

---

75 SG: Grammar: feminine plural.
76 SG: Grammar: feminine plural.
77 SG: Grammar: dual.
78 SG: Grammar: dual.
79 SG: Grammar: dual.
80 SG: i.e. four lunar months and ten days.

with them secretly save that you speak a fitting word. And do not decide upon the knot of marriage until the writ reaches its term. And know that God knows what is within your souls, so fear Him. And know that God is forgiving and clement.
(2:234-235)

Divorce process in case you have not touched the women

O you who heed warning: when you marry believing women then divorce them before you have touched them: there is no number for you that you should count concerning them; but give them provision, and release them with a comely release.
(33:49)

You do no wrong if you divorce women when you have neither touched them nor appointed for them an obligation. But make them a gift: the wealthy according to his means, and the straitened according to his means; a provision according to what is fitting is binding upon the doers of good.

And if you divorce them before you have touched them and you have already appointed for them an obligation, then half of what you appointed unless they forgo it, or he in whose hand is the knot of marriage forgoes it; and that you forgo is nearer to prudent fear. And forget not bounty between you, God sees what you do.
(2:236-237)

Count the waiting period and take witnesses

O Prophet: when you divorce women, divorce them after their waiting period; and count the waiting period,[81] and be in prudent fear of God, your Lord. Turn them

---
81 SM: See 2:226-228.

not out of their houses, nor let them go forth save if they commit manifest sexual immorality. And those are the limits of God; and whoso transgresses the limits of God has wronged his soul. Thou knowest not, that God might, after that, bring about a new matter.

And when they have reached their term, retain them according to what is fitting, or release them according to what is fitting. And call to witness two just men from among you; and uphold the witness for God.[82] By that is admonished he who believes in God and the Last Day; and whoso is in prudent fear of God — He will make for him a way out,

And He will provide for him from where he reckoned not. And whoso places his trust in God, He is sufficient for him. God achieves His purpose; God has appointed a measure for all things.

And for such of your women as despair of menstruation, if you doubt,[83] their waiting period is three months, as well as for those who have not menstruated.[84] And for those who are bearing, their waiting period is until they lay down their burden. And whoso is in prudent fear of God — He will make for him, of His command, ease.

That is the command of God that He sent down to you; and whoso is in prudent fear of God — He will remove from him his evil deeds and make great for him his reward.

Let them dwell in what manner you dwell, out of your means, and harm them not so as to straiten them. And

---

82 SG: As part of the divorce process, after the waiting period — no matter what the outcome — the decision should be witnessed, whereafter those involved are to abide by that which has been witnessed.

83 SM: That they may be pregnant.

84 SG: Often said by the Traditionalist — on the basis of his library of dubious fiction — to mean female children who have not started menstruation. To those who claim that the mood is perfect under the influence of lam (i.e. who have not yet[...]) I would point out that the relative pronoun and the verb are in the feminine plural and refer to (in fact, can only refer to) women (Arabic: nisā') in the preceding clause. The Qur'an speaks of women as legally competent females (who can own property, take oaths, bear witness, swear fealty, incur punishment for crimes). Minors can do none of those things. Cases of women not menstruating while not pregnant are not unusual, and it is this which is referenced here.

if they be bearing, then spend on them until they lay down their burden. Then if they suckle for you, then give them their reward, and take counsel among you according to what is fitting. And if there be difficulties between you, another shall suckle for him.

Let him who has abundance spend out of his abundance, and whose provision is measured — let him spend out of what God has given him. God charges not a soul save with what He has given it. God will make, after hardship, ease.

(65:1-7)

Make provision for wives and ex-wives

And those among you who die and leave wives is a bequest for their wives: provision for a year without expulsion. But if they go forth,[85] you do no wrong in what they do concerning themselves according to what is fitting; and God is exalted in might and wise.

And for divorced women provision according to what is fitting is binding upon those of prudent fear.

(2:240-241)

Do not hold onto denying women

O you who heed warning: when the believing women come to you as émigrées: examine them. God best knows their faith. And if you know them to be believing women, then return them not to the atheists. Such women are not lawful for them, and they are not lawful for such women. And give them[86] what they spent. And you do no wrong to marry such women when you give them their rewards.[87] And hold not by tie denying women; and ask for what you have spent, and let them[88] ask

---
85 SG: i.e. if they leave after provision has been made for them.
86 SG: i.e. the atheists. Grammar: masculine plural object pronoun.
87 SM: A man must pay an amount to the woman.
88 SG: i.e. the atheists.

for what they have spent. That is the judgment of God;
He judges between you; and God is knowing and wise.
(60:10)

As we go through the Writ of God, you will notice a common theme: God's commands are not only practical but also just. Unlike the divorce process in the West which leans heavily in favor of the woman, God's Writ protects the rights of all three parties: husband, wife and child.

We shall now look at the subject of inheritance in the writ of God.

4
INHERITANCE

And let those fear who, if they left behind them weak progeny, would be afraid for them; so let them be in prudent fear of God, and speak an apposite word. (4:9)

The right to bequest

While God's Writ ordains a bequest for parents and relatives, according to what is fitting, it also lays down fixed percentages to be distributed among near relatives. In the case of children, the Writ regarding inheritance is explicit: they must receive their God-ordained percentages before any other disbursement of funds (i.e. a bequest or settlement of debt can only be executed after a deceased's children get their God-ordained share). See section *Working Example* at the end of this chapter.

Prescribed for you when death is present with one of you, if he leaves wealth: the bequest to parents and relatives according to what is fitting[89] is binding upon those of prudent fear.
And whoso changes it after he hears it, the sin thereof is only upon those who change it; God is hearing and knowing.

---

89 SM: or *suitable* i.e. a dying believer must allot wealth to parents and relatives (a bequest). However, the God-ordained fixed percentages (as per 4:11-12) must be given too.

But whoso fears from a testator partiality or sin and makes right between them, no sin is upon him; God is forgiving and merciful.
(2:180-182)

O you who heed warning: a witness between you when death approaches one of you at the time of bequest is two just men among you; or two others from other than yourselves if you are travelling in the earth when the calamity of death befalls you. Detain them after the duty,[90] and they shall swear by God, if you doubt: "We would not sell it for a price,[91] though he were a relative, nor will we conceal the witness of God; then would we be among the sinners."
But if it be found that they have laid claim in sin, then two others shall stand in their place — the two foremost from those that lay claim — and let them swear by God: "Our witness is worthier than their witness; and we have not transgressed: then would we be among the wrongdoers."
That will tend to them bearing witness properly, or fearing that oaths will be taken after their oaths. And be in prudent fear of God, and listen; and God guides not the perfidious people.
(5:106-108)

God-ordained shares for relatives

To men belongs a share of what parents and relatives leave; and to women belongs a share of what parents and relatives leave — from what is little thereof or much — a share ordained.[92]

---

90 SM: After you have discharged your duty of bequeathing as per 2:180.
91 SG: i.e. that they are not bribed or in any way suborned to say what is not true.
92 SM: My understanding is that all parties that stand to inherit per 4:11-12 must get *something* (i.e. a bequest or settlement of debts cannot exhaust all wealth before it can be distributed to relatives). The inheritance of children is explicitly safeguarded. See note to 4:11.

And when present at the division are relatives, and the fatherless, and the poor: give to them therefrom; and speak to them a fitting word.

And let those fear who, if they left behind them weak progeny, would be afraid for them; so let them be in prudent fear of God, and speak an apposite word.

Those who consume the property of the fatherless unjustly:[93] they but consume into their bellies Fire; and they will burn in an inferno.

God charges you concerning your children: for the male is the like of the portion of two females;[94] but if there are women above two, then for them is two-thirds of what he[95] left; and if she is one,[96] then for her is half;[97] and for his parents: for each one of them is one-sixth of what he left if he has a child.[98] Then if he has not a child[99] and there inherit from him his parents, for his mother is one-third; but if he has brothers or sisters: for his mother is one-sixth, after a bequest he has made, or debt — your parents and your children: you know not which of them is nearer to you in benefit — as an obligation from God; God is knowing and wise.

And for you is half of what your wives left if they have not a child;[100] but if they have a child,[101] then for you is one-fourth of what they left, after a bequest they have made, or debt. And for them:[102] one-fourth of what you

---

93 SM: A warning to safeguard the portion of the deceased's children.
94 SM: for example, if the deceased had three daughters and a son, the son would receive a share equal to two daughters. See *Working Example* below.
95 SG: i.e. the deceased.
96 SM: in the case of only two girls, we can deduce (using 4:176) that for them is two-thirds of what he left.
97 SM: notice that the phrase "after a bequest he has made, or debt" does not occur in the case of children i.e. a bequest or settlement of debt can only be executed after the children are given their God-ordained shares.
98 SM: or *children*.
99 SM: or *children*.
100 SM: or *children*.
101 SM: or *children*.
102 SM: your wives.

left, if you have not a child;[103] but if you have a child:[104] for them[105] is one-eighth of what you left, after a bequest you have made, or debt. And if a man or a woman be inherited with no immediate heir[106] but has a brother or sister, for each of them is one-sixth; but if they are more than that, then are they partners in one-third, after a bequest he has made, or debt, without harm, as a bequest from God; and God is knowing and clement.
Those are the limits of God. And whoso obeys God and His messenger, He will make him enter gardens beneath which rivers flow, they abiding eternally therein; and that is the Great Achievement.
(4:7-13)

And for all have We appointed heirs to what parents and relatives leave; and those with whom you have entered into contract:[107] give them their share; God is witness over all things.
(4:33)

They ask thee for a ruling. Say thou: "God gives you the ruling concerning those without an immediate heir: if a man perishes without a child[108] but has a sister: for her is half of what he left, and he inherits from her if she has not a child.[109] But if there are two females: for them is two-thirds of what he left. And if they are brethren, men and women: for the male is the like of the share of two females." And God makes plain to you lest you go astray; and God knows all things.
(4:176)

---

103 SM: or *children*.
104 SM: or *children*.
105 SM: your wives.
106 SG: Arabic: *kalāla* — *without an immediate heir*. Said to mean one without living parent or child; judging from the preceding context one might argue that the category also encompasses a living spouse. See also 4:176.
107 SM: I take this to mean *your wives* or *your debtors*.
108 SM: or *children*.
109 SM: or *children*.

Working Example

At the time of his death, Ahmad had $15,000 to his name. On his death bed, he left the following bequest amounts to his family:

Son: $300
Daughter 1: $200
Daughter 2: $200
Wife: $1000
Father: $700
Mother: $400

Ahmad also had an outstanding debt of $750.

Starting inheritance amount: $15,000

As per 4:11, his children get their God-ordained share first before the execution of his bequest or settlement of debt. His son gets a share equivalent to two of his daughters.[110] Therefore, for calculation purposes, we will assume Ahmad had four daughters (a male gets a portion of two females). Total share to be split between these assumed four daughters is $10,000 (⅔ X $15,000). His son gets $5000 (the share of two females) and his two daughters get $2500 each.

Remaining Inheritance amount: $5000 ($15,000 - $10,000)

Next, we execute Ahmad's bequest and pay off his outstanding debt. His son gets $300 on top of his God-ordained share. Similarly his two daughters get $200 each. His wife gets $1000. His father gets $700 and his mother gets $400. His debtor is paid $750.

Remaining Inheritance amount: $1450 ($5000 - $3550)

Next, we apply rules in 4:11-12 to distribute the God-ordained amounts to his wife and parents.

---

110 SM: "...for the male is the like of the portion of two females;.." (2:11)

His parents get $241.66 (⅙ X $1450) each in addition to what they got in the bequest earlier.

Remaining Inheritance amount: $966.68 ($1450- $483.32)

His wife gets $120.84 (⅛ X $966.68) in addition to what she got in the bequest earlier.

The remaining inheritance of $845.84 ($966.68 - $120.84) would then be distributed to other relatives, the fatherless and poor at the time of the division.[111]

As mentioned earlier, the *Sharia* Law in regards to inheritance has a whole host of stipulations and exclusions which are not found in the Writ of God. To deny the deceased's children their God-ordained shares based on man-made technicalities is something for which the criminals will have to answer for on the Day of Judgment.

We shall now look at what the Writ of God has to say about food.

---

[111] SM: Per 4:8.

5
FOOD

Say thou: "Who has made unlawful the adornment of God which He brought forth for His servants, and the good things of provision?" Say thou: "These are for those who heed warning in the life of this world exclusively on the Day of Resurrection." Thus do We set out and detail the proofs for people who know.
(7:32)

Intoxicants

They ask thee about wine[112] and games of chance. Say thou: "In both is great sin, and benefits for men; but their sin is greater than their benefit." And they ask thee what they should spend. Say thou: "The surplus." Thus does God make plain to you the proofs, that you might reflect
(2:219)

O you who heed warning: wine, and games of chance, and altars, and divining arrows are an abomination of the work of the satan; so avoid it, that you might be successful.
The satan but wishes to cause between you enmity and hatred in wine and the games of chance, and to turn you

---

112 SM: See a full list of verses where this word occurs: 2:219, 5:90, 5:91, 12:36, 12:41, 47:15.

away from the remembrance of God and from the duty; so will you not desist?
(5:90-91)

General rules

O mankind: eat of what is in the earth lawful and good, and follow not the footsteps of the satan; he is to you an open enemy.
(2:168)

O you who heed warning: eat of the good things that We have provided you; and be grateful to God if it be Him you serve.
He has only made unlawful to you carrion,[113] and blood, and the flesh of swine, and that dedicated to other than God. But whoso is forced, neither desiring nor transgressing, no sin is upon him; God is forgiving and merciful.
(2:172-173)

In my view, a believer living in the West can consume chicken and seafood from factory slaughterhouses[114] since they are not going against the general rules in 2:173. However, there are special rules for grazing livestock (cow, goat, camel etc.) which makes their meat supplied by regular factory slaughterhouses unfit for consumption by a believer.

Special rules regarding grazing livestock

A believer must follow additional rules (in addition to the rules of not consuming carrion, blood, flesh of swine and dedication to other than God) in the case of grazing livestock. In the U.S, captive-bolt stunning is used during the livestock slaughtering process. In a nutshell, this process involves blunt force trauma to the animal's head using a special gun (bolt gun) thereby "stunning" it. It is a matter of debate

---

113 SM: See 6:139 where this word is used in case of a stillbirth i.e. an animal that died of natural causes.
114 SM: i.e. factories that distribute to retail grocery stores (Walmart, Tesco, utility stores).

whether the animal is rendered unconscious or killed after undergoing said "stunning". Regardless, striking livestock on the head with a bolt is *beating* the animal which, in my view, violates the injunction to not beat an animal in 5:3.

The Islamic ritual slaughter method[115] is suspect as well because it does not explicitly prohibit captive-bolt stunning which, as mentioned previously, in my view renders an animal forbidden as per 5:3

For a believer living in the U.S., Kosher meat is the safest option because the *shechita*[116] method is in line with the special rules laid down in 5:3.

> That[...]. And whoso honours the sacred things of God, it is better for him in the sight of his Lord. And the cattle are lawful to you save that recited to you.[117] And avoid the abomination of idols. And avoid false speech,
> Inclining towards God, not ascribing a partnership to Him. And whoso ascribes a partnership to God, it is as if he had fallen from the sky, then the birds snatch him away, or the wind sweeps him away to a far-off place. (22:30-31)

> O you who heed warning: fulfil contracts. Made lawful for you is grazing livestock[118] save what is recited to you,[119] hunting not being permitted when you are forbidden; God ordains what He wills.
> O you who heed warning: violate not the tokens of God, nor the inviolable month, nor the offering, nor the necklaces, nor the visitors to the inviolable house seeking the favour of their Lord and approval. And when you are permitted, then you may hunt. And let not hatred of a people who turned you away from the inviolable place

---

115 SM: Termed *dhabihah*.
116 SM: https://en.wikipedia.org/wiki/Shechita
117 SM: See 5:3 below.
118 SM: A quadraped. See 6:143-144 for examples.
119 SM: i.e. in the case of grazing livestock, the rules in 5:3 are to be followed.

of worship move you to commit injustice. And assist one another to virtue and prudent fear; and assist not one another in sin and enmity. And be in prudent fear of God; God is severe in retribution.

Forbidden to you is carrion, and blood, and the flesh of swine, and that dedicated to other than God, and the strangled, and the beaten,[120] and the fallen, and the gored, and that eaten by the beast of prey save what you slaughter, and that sacrificed upon the altar,[121] and that you seek apportionment by divining arrows — that is perfidy — (this day have those who ignore warning despaired of your doctrine, so fear them not, but fear Me; this day have I perfected for you your doctrine and completed My favour upon you, and approved for you submission as doctrine) but whoso is compelled by hunger, without inclination to sin — God is forgiving and merciful.

They ask thee what is made lawful for them. Say thou: "Made lawful for you are good things; and what you have trained of animals of prey as trainers[122] teaching them of what God taught you — eat of what they catch for you, and remember the name of God over it. And be in prudent fear of God; God is swift in reckoning."

This day are good things made lawful for you; and the food of those given the Writ is lawful for you,[123] and your food is lawful for them, as are chaste women among the believing women and chaste women among those given the Writ before you, when you have given them their dowries, being chaste and not fornicators, nor taking

---

120 SM: Slaughterhouses in the U.S. use captive-bolt stunning, a procedure which boils down to hitting the animal forcefully on the head.
121 SM: Arberry translates as *sacrificed to idols*.
122 SG: Arabic: *mukallibīn* — *trainers*. This word is from the root *k-l-b* from which comes *kalb* (dog). Understood here is the use of hunting animals such as dogs and falcons. The Traditionalist's treatment of dogs as unclean is found nowhere in the Qur'an (cf. 18:18, 18:22).
123 SM: Because they are following the same Writ.

secret friends. And whoso denies the faith: his work has been in vain, and he in the Hereafter is among the losers. (5:1-5)

O you who heed warning: forbid not the good things that God has made lawful for you;[124] and transgress not; God loves not the transgressors.
And eat of what God has provided you, lawful and good; and be in prudent fear of God in whom you are believers. (5:87-88)

Those who heed warning and do righteous deeds do no wrong in what they eat when they are in prudent fear and believe and do righteous deeds. Then be in prudent fear and believe! Then be in prudent fear and do righteous deeds! And God loves the doers of good. (5:93)

Made lawful for you is the game of the sea and the food thereof, as a provision for you and for those who travel; but forbidden to you is the game of the land so long as you are forbidden;[125] and be in prudent fear of God to whom you will be gathered. (5:96)

Remember God's name over what you eat

And for every community We appointed a rite: that they remember the name of God over what He has provided them of livestock cattle.[126] And your God is One God; so submit to Him. And bear thou glad tidings to the humble:

---

124 SG: Lamentably, the stock-in-trade of the Traditionalist stands in precise opposition to this exhortation. He has an entire library of things he forbids or enjoins, various combinations and interpretations of which are presented and accepted as a religion called Islam.
125 SM: This in context of visiting the inviolable house of worship. See 5:1-2.
126 SG: The Traditionalist's stock-in-trade is (what one might call sectarian) rite and dogma. As he himself acknowledges, the Qur'an is conspicuously lacking in both. Here, however, we are given a single rite with enough detail to allow us to implement it, and in a context which speaks of every community. On this basis we may reasonably assume

Whose hearts are afraid when God is remembered, and those patient over what befalls them, and who uphold the duty, and of what We have provided them they spend.

And the camels: We appointed them for you among the tokens of God; for you in them is good. So remember the name of God over them when they are in lines; and when their flanks collapse, eat thereof and feed the reticent poor and the beggar. Thus have We made them subject for you, that you might be grateful.

(22:34-36)

So eat of that over which the name of God has been remembered, if you believe in His proofs.

And what is with you that you eat not of that over which the name of God has been remembered when He has set out and detailed to you what is forbidden you save that you be compelled thereto? And many lead astray by their vain desires,[127] without knowledge;[128] thy Lord: He best knows the transgressors.

And leave the outwardness of sin and the inwardness thereof; those who earn sin will be rewarded with what they committed.

---

that we are to keep this rite. This point is confirmed at 22:67. See also note to 22:30. Here, for the usual reasons, the Traditionalist frequently attempts to interpolate his required conclusions into the text; Saheeh International, for example, has: And for all religion We have appointed a rite [of sacrifice] that they may mention the name of Allāh over what He has provided for them of [sacrificial] animals. This is a deceit on at least three counts. Firstly, ummah is translated by him (usually) as community and not religion; secondly, he has inserted 'sacrificial' next to 'rite' where it does not exist; thirdly, he has inserted 'sacrificial' next to 'animals' where it does not exist. The word he translates animals here (Arabic: al an'ām) occurs 33 times in the text (3:14, 4:119, 5:1, 5:95, 6:136, 6:138, 6:138, 6:138, 6:139, 6:142, 7:179, 10:24, 16:5, 16:66, 16:80, 20:54, 22:28, 22:30, 22:34, 23:21, 25:44, 25:49, 26:133, 32:27, 35:28, 36:71, 39:6, 40:79, 42:11, 43:12, 47:12, 79:33, 80:32). In no other case does he claim the reference to be to 'sacrificial' animals.

127 SG: See *vain desires* at 2:78, 2:111, 2:120, 2:145, 4:123, 4:123, 5:48, 5:49, 5:77, 6:56, 6:119, 6:150, 13:37, 23:71, 28:50, 30:29, 42:15, 45:18, 47:14, 47:16, 54:3, 57:14.

128 SG: This description includes the Traditionalist who is not satisfied with the clear dietary laws in the Qur'an, and has a plethora of additional and complicated rules he seeks to make binding upon himself and others.

And eat not of that over which the name of God has not been remembered; and it is perfidy. And the satans instruct their allies to dispute with you; and if you obey them, you are idolaters.
(6:118-121)

And He it is that produces gardens, trellised and untrellised, and the date-palms, and crops diverse in their food, and the olive and the pomegranate, similar yet different. Eat of the fruit thereof when it bears fruit, and render its due on the day of its harvest; and commit not excess, He loves not the committers of excess.
And of the cattle for burden and for skin: eat of what God has provided you, and follow not the footsteps of the satan; he is an open enemy to you.
(6:141-142)

Do not forbid what God has allowed and vice-versa

"Eight pairs:[129] of sheep two and of goats two--" Say thou: "Is it the two males He has forbidden or the two females? If what the wombs of the two females contain:[130] inform me with knowledge, if you be truthful."
"And of camels two and of oxen two--" Say thou: "Is it the two males He has forbidden or the two females? If[131] what the wombs of the two females contain: — or if you were witnesses when God enjoined this upon you: — then who is more unjust than he who invents a lie about God, that he might lead people astray without knowledge? God guides not the wrongdoing people."
Say thou: "I find not in what has been revealed to me what is unlawful to one who would eat it save it be carrion, or blood poured forth, or the flesh of swine — and it is an abomination — or perfidy dedicated to other than God";

---

129 SM: Examples of animals belonging to the category of grazing livestock alluded to in 5:1.
130 SG: i.e. if this is the claim.
131 SG: i.e. if this is the claim.

but whoso is forced, neither desiring nor transgressing: thy Lord is forgiving and merciful.

And to those who hold to Judaism We made unlawful every animal with a claw; and of oxen and sheep We made unlawful to them the fat thereof save what their backs bear, or the entrails, or what is mixed with bone; that We rewarded them for their sectarian zealotry; and We are truthful.

And if they deny thee, say thou: "Your Lord is the Possessor of Mercy; but not repelled is His wrath from the lawbreaking people."

(6:143-147)

So eat of what God has provided you, lawful and good; and be grateful for the favour of your Lord if it be Him you serve.

He has but made unlawful to you carrion, and blood, and the flesh of swine, and that dedicated to other than God; but whoso is forced, neither desiring nor transgressing: God is forgiving and merciful.

And add not to what your tongues describe the lie: "This is lawful, and this is unlawful," to invent lies about God; those who invent lies about God will not succeed:

A brief enjoyment, and they have a painful punishment.

And to those who hold to Judaism We made unlawful what We related to thee before;[132] and We wronged them not, but they wronged their souls.

(16:114-118)

We shall now look at what the Writ of God has to say about the fatherless.

---

[132] SM: See 6:146.

6
FATHERLESS

> Then as for the fatherless: oppress thou not.
> (93:9)

The Qur'an uses the term *yatama* to mean *children/adults without fathers*. Typical translations use the term *orphan* for this Arabic word. This is problematic for two reasons:

1. It diminishes the importance of a father in a family structure; the Qur'an lays great importance on the role of a man as the head of the household
2. The commands applicable for *children/adults without fathers* would then be limited to only *children/adults without parents*

To mitigate these issues, it is better to translate *yatama* as *fatherless* to better keep in line with how the Qur'an uses this term. Brother Gerrans, in his translation, uses the term *fatherless* instead of *orphans*.

> They ask thee about wine and games of chance. Say thou: "In both is great sin, and benefits for men; but their sin is greater than their benefit." And they ask thee what they should spend. Say thou: "The surplus." Thus does God make plain to you the proofs, that you might reflect Upon the World and the Hereafter. And they ask thee about the fatherless. Say thou: "Improvement for them is best." And if you associate with them, then are they

your brothers.¹³³ And God knows the worker of corruption from the doer of right. And had God willed, He would have caused distress for you;¹³⁴ God is exalted in might and wise.
(2:219-220)

Marry up to four fatherless women

O mankind:¹³⁵ be in prudent fear of your Lord who created you from one soul; and created from it its mate, and scattered from them many men and women; and be in prudent fear of God through whom, and through kinship, you ask one of another; God is over you, watching.

And give the fatherless¹³⁶ their property;¹³⁷ and exchange not the bad for the good, nor consume their property into your property;¹³⁸ that is a great misdeed.

And if you fear that you will not do justice¹³⁹ by the fatherless, then marry what pleases you of women:¹⁴⁰ two or three or four.¹⁴¹ But if you fear that you will not do justice,¹⁴² then one — or what your right hands possess; that is more likely that you will not deviate.¹⁴³ (4:1-3)

---

133 SM: Arberry translates as: "Say: 'To set their affairs aright is good. And if you intermix with them, they are your brothers;'". I understand it to mean that they can be adopted with the caveat that we not claim them to be our sons or daughters. See 58:2, 33:4-5.
134 SM: By laying down more stringent laws in regards to the fatherless.
135 SM: This directive is to all mankind, not just to the believers.
136 SG: Arabic: *yatāmā (pl.) yatīm (sg.)* — *orphan, fatherless*. I render as fatherless throughout since the context treats in many places of those who have been either abandoned by fathers, are of unknown parentage, or whose fathers have been killed in battle. All instances appear in the notes and reference this verse.
137 SM: If they are mature, otherwise safeguard it until they reach maturity. See 4:6.
138 SM: i.e. maintain separate accounts.
139 SM: This is a form IV of the verb *qasata* which means *to act justly, in fairness, equitably*. I take this to mean that if you fear you cannot uphold the directives in the previous verse.
140 SG: The word here is *nisā'* (women) which always indicates adult, legally competent females.
141 SM: Lit: twos, threes or fours. It is clear that polygamy is only allowed if we fear we cannot do justice by the fatherless. See also 4:127.
142 SM: the Arabic word is *adala* which in this context means to not treat equally.
143 SG: i.e. from the right course. Arabic: *'āla* — to deviate from the right course; to oppress, distress (someone), weigh heavily (upon) (Wehr, p. 770). This is the only instance

The above verse (4:3) is used by Muslims to justify wholesale polygamy; however a careful reading reveals that it allows polygamy in a specific circumstance: where there is a glut of fatherless women (possibly because of a war) and something needs to be done about it. In this scenario, a man[144] (who has assumed their guardianship) can marry two, three or four of these fatherless *women* if he fears he cannot safeguard their financial interests as per 4:3.[145] But if he feels he will not be equitable to all of them then he can only marry one fatherless woman.[146] This is the plain reading of this verse. I struggle to understand how a believing man currently living in the West can use this verse to justify marrying two, three or four women.

> And give the women their dowries as a gift willingly;[147] but if they remit to you anything of it voluntarily, then consume it with satisfaction and pleasure.
> (4:4)

> And they ask thee for a ruling concerning women. Say thou: "God[148] gives you the ruling concerning them," — and what is recited to you[149] in the Writ concerning the fatherless women (to whom you give not what is prescribed for them,[150] and yet desire to marry them) and concerning the oppressed among children; and that

---

of this root in the text.
144 SM: This injunction begins with "O mankind" which makes it clear that it is not just directed to the believers only.
145 SM: "...stand up for equity for the fatherless..." (4:127) and "And if you fear that you will not do justice by the fatherless..." (4:3).
146 SM: Or *what his right hands possess*. I, as noted earlier, ignore this group.
147 SM: Just because they are fatherless does not mean that a believer can forego on giving them their rightful payment.
148 SG: It is not for the Messenger to make rulings; he follows what God gives; cf. 4:176.
149 SG: They already have an answer (4:3-6). This section illustrates the archetypal, incorrect attitude towards Muḥammad — that of asking him for rulings. The Messenger cannot give rulings; the ruling is from God. This section (4:127-134) has a chiding tone: restating patiently points which have been made, repeatedly stating that all that is in the heavens and the earth belongs to God, and closing with the observation that God can replace the recipients of the message at any time with another people.
150 SM: i.e. their payment. See 4:4.

you stand up for equity for the fatherless. And whatever you do of good, God knows it.

But if a woman fears contempt or aversion from her husband, they do no wrong that they do right between themselves in peace; and making right is better; and avarice is present in the souls. But if you do good and are in prudent fear, then is God aware of what you do.

And you will not be able to deal equally between wives, though you be desirous; but turn not entirely away leaving one as if suspended. And if you do right and are in prudent fear, God is forgiving and merciful.

But if they part, God will enrich each out of His abundance; and God is encompassing and wise.

(4:127-130)

Deliver the fatherless' property to him when he has reached maturity/marriage

And give not the foolish[151] your wealth which God gave you as sustenance, but feed them and clothe them out of it;[152] and speak to them a fitting word.

And test[153] the fatherless when they have reached marriage: if you find them to be of sound judgment, deliver to them their property; and consume it not[154] wastefully and hastily before they be grown. And he that is free from need, let him abstain; and he that is poor, let him take[155] according to what is fitting. And when you deliver to them their property, take witnesses over them. And sufficient is God as reckoner.

(4:5-6)

Keeping the directive, "And approach not the property of the

---

151 SG: i.e. incompetent.
152 SM: Feed and clothe them out of your property; not theirs. See discussion below.
153 SG: i.e. to see if they are ready for the responsibilities of manhood.
154 SM: I take this to mean to not waste the fatherless' inheritance on his frivolous needs.
155 SG: Lit.: *consume, eat.*

fatherless save with what is better before he reaches his maturity..."[156] in mind, the directive: "...and he that is poor, let him take according to what is fitting..."[157] does not mean (as is commonly thought) that a guardian can use the fatherless' inheritance to *pay himself* or *offset the costs of upkeep of the fatherless*. The fatherless' inheritance must be kept in a separate account.[158] However, when the fatherless has reached the age of marriage/maturity, a poor guardian can take a due payment "according to what is fitting". The fatherless will now also be at an age where he can understand (and appreciate) such a transaction.

Safeguard fatherless' property until they reach maturity/marriage

"And approach not the property of the fatherless save with what is better before he reaches his maturity; and fulfil the measure and the balance with equity," — We burden not any soul save to its capacity — "and when you speak, be just (though he be a relative); and the covenant of God fulfil; — that He commanded you, that you might take heed."
(6:152)

And approach not the property of the fatherless save with what is better before he reaches maturity. And fulfil the covenant; the covenant is to be questioned.
(17:34)

Those who consume the property of the fatherless unjustly: they but consume into their bellies Fire; and they will burn in an inferno.
(4:10)

---

156 SM: "'And approach not the property of the fatherless save with what is better before he reaches his maturity; and fulfil the measure and the balance with equity,' — We burden not any soul save to its capacity — 'and when you speak, be just (though he be a relative); and the covenant of God fulfil; — that He commanded you, that you might take heed.'" (6:152)
157 SM: See 4:6 above.
158 SM: See 4:2.

It is a great misdeed to consume the property of the fatherless unjustly. Any religious ruling or State Law which permits a guardian (or any other party) to consume the property of the fatherless is in direct violation of God's Writ.

We shall now look at what the Writ of God has to say about commercial dealings.

7
COMMERCE

And the heaven — He raised it (and He set up the balance,
That you transgress not in the balance;
And uphold the weight with equity, and cause not loss to the balance.)
(55:7-9)

Do not defraud others

And consume not your wealth among yourselves in vanity, neither offer it to the authorities that you might consume part of the property of the people through sin, when you know.
(2:188)

O you who heed warning: consume not your wealth among yourselves in vanity, or save by way of trade by mutual consent among you; and kill not yourselves;[159] God is merciful to you;
And whoso does that in enmity and injustice, him will We burn in a Fire; and that is easy for God.
If you avoid the enormities of what you are forbidden, We will remove from you your evil deeds and make you enter at a noble entrance.
(4:29-31)

---

159 SG: I have rendered literally. Arguments are made in favour of: *Kill some among you*; cf. 2:54, 2:85, 4:29, 4:66.

Woe to the unfair traders:[160] —
Those who, when they take measure from men, take in full,
But when they give them by measure or give them by weight, cause loss.
Do those not think that they will be raised
To a tremendous day: —
A day men will stand before the Lord of All Creation?
(83:1-6)

Do not consume usury

Those who consume usury will not stand save as stands he whom the satan buffets with his touch;[161] for it is that they say: "Commerce is but the same as usury,"[162] when God has made commerce lawful and forbidden usury! And he to whom came the admonition from his Lord, and desisted: he has what is past, and his case is with God. But whoso returns: those are the companions of the Fire; therein they abide eternally.

God eliminates usury, and increases charity; and God loves not every ingrate and sinner.

Those who heed warning and do righteous deeds, and uphold the duty, and render the purity: they have their reward with their Lord; and no fear will be upon them, nor will they grieve.

O you who heed warning: be in prudent fear of God; and give up what remains of usury, if you be believers.

And if you do not, then be informed of war from God and His messenger. But if you repent, then to you are your principal sums; doing no wrong, you will not be wronged.

---

160 SG: **Qur'anic definition:** *muṭaffifūn*. The definition is provided at verses 83:2-3 which is, in summary, that they take from men in full but cause loss when they give. This value is rendered variously (and correctly) by Traditionalist translators as *stinters, those who give less than is due,* or *those who deal in fraud*.

161 SG: Lit.: *of the touch*; i.e. one in whom normal functioning has been replaced by affliction or possession.

162 SM: i.e. you profit in both cases.

> And if he[163] be one in hardship, then deferment until ease; but that you forgive by way of charity is better for you, if you would know.
> (2:275-280)

While moderns make a distinction between *usury* and *interest*, the God's Writ considers any profit earned on a loan to be *raba*.[164] We can validate this understanding by looking closely at 2:279: "...But if you repent, then to you are your principal sums...". Thus *any* profit made on money (principal sum) loaned to men is not allowed in the Writ of God. To put it another way, *interest* and *usury* are both forbidden since they are essentially the same thing: proceeds from an unjust transaction.

> O you who heed warning: consume not usury, doubled and redoubled; and be in prudent fear of God, that you might be successful.
> (3:130)

> Have they not considered that God expands provision for whom He wills, and He straitens? In that are proofs for people who believe.
> So give thou the relative his due, and the needy, and the wayfarer. That is best for those who desire the face of God; and it is they who are the successful.
> And what you give of usury that it might increase in the wealth of men,[165] there is no increase with God; but what you give of purity, desiring the face of God: it is they who receive recompense manifold.
> (30:37-39)

Rules for contracting a debt

> O you who heed warning: when you contract a debt together to a stated term: write it down, and let a writer

---
163 SG: i.e. one who owes you money.
164 SM: *Raba*: to increase; to grow. (Hans-Wehr)
165 SM: Using the proceeds from a usurious loan as an investment for the next financial scheme; see also 3:130.

write it down between you justly; and let not a writer refuse to write it down as God has taught him; so let him write, and let the debtor[166] dictate, and let him be in prudent fear of God, his Lord, and diminish nothing thereof. But if the debtor[167] be incompetent,[168] or weak, or unable to dictate himself, then his ally shall dictate justly. And call to witness two witnesses from among your men; but if there be not two men, then a man and two women among those you approve as witnesses, that should one of them err, one of them might remind the other; and let not the witnesses refuse when they are called. And be not weary of writing it, small or great, with its term (that is more just in the sight of God, and more upright for witness, and likelier that there will be no doubt between you) save if it be present trade that you transact among you;[169] then you do no wrong that you write it not down. And take witnesses when you enter into contract.[170] And let not a writer or witness be harmed. And if you do, then is it perfidy among you. And be in prudent fear of God. And God is teaching you; and God knows all things.

And if you are on a journey, and find not a writer, then: a pledge in hand.[171] But if one of you trusts another, then let him who is trusted discharge his trust, and let him be in prudent fear of God, his Lord. And conceal not the witness; and he who conceals it, his heart is sinful; and God knows what you do.

To God belongs what is in the heavens and what is in the earth; whether you reveal what is within yourselves or hide it, God will call you to account for it. And He forgives

---

166 SG: Lit.: *he upon whom is the obligation*. Arabic: *al ḥaqq*. See Notepad XVII (al ḥaqq ii.).
167 SG: Lit.: *he upon whom is the obligation*. Arabic: *al ḥaqq*. See Notepad XVII (al ḥaqq ii.).
168 SM: Arberry translates as *fool*.
169 SM: i.e. it is an immediate transaction between you.
170 SM: Arberry translates as *trafficking one with another*.
171 SM: I take this to mean that a security deposit can be taken in lieu of a written agreement if a writer is not found.

whom He wills, and punishes whom He wills; and God is over all things powerful.
(2:282-284)

Be honest in your financial dealings

And among the doctors of the Law is he who, if thou entrust him with a fortune, will deliver it to thee. And among them is he who, if thou entrust him with a dinar, will not return it to thee unless thou stand over him. For it is that they say: "We owe nothing to the unschooled"; and they ascribe the lie to God, when they know!
Verily, whoso fulfils his covenant and is in prudent fear: God loves those of prudent fear.
Those who sell the covenant of God and their oaths at a cheap price: those have no portion in the Hereafter; and God will not speak to them or look at them on the Day of Resurrection, nor will He increase them in purity. And they have a painful punishment.
(3:75-77)

And covet not that wherein God has favoured some of you over others. For men is a share of what they have earned, and for women is a share of what they have earned. And ask God of His bounty; God is knower of all things.
And for all have We appointed heirs to what parents and relatives leave; and those with whom you have entered into contract: give them their share; God is witness over all things.
(4:32-33)

God has forbidden the taking of interest. Sadly, the financial system of today is rife with this forbidden practice. The Muslims of today, who claim to hold fast to the Writ of God, have also now fully embraced and implemented the usurious financial system of the West; to the ruin of all.

We shall now look at what the Writ of God has to say about retaliation.

8
RETALIATION

And fight in the cause of God those who fight you, but transgress not; God loves not the transgressors. (2:190)

Retaliate in equal measure

O you who heed warning: just requital is ordained for you concerning those killed: the freeman for the freeman, and the slave for the slave, and the female for the female. But whoso is pardoned anything by his brother,[172] let the pursuance be according to what is fitting and the payment to him with good conduct; that is an alleviation and mercy from your Lord. And whoso transgresses after that, he has a painful punishment.
And there is life for you in just requital, O you men of understanding, that you might be in prudent fear.[173] (2:178-179)

The inviolable month is for the inviolable month, and the inviolable deeds are just requital: whoso transgressed against you, transgress against him just as he transgressed against you. But be in prudent fear of God, and know that God is with those of prudent fear. (2:194)

---
172 SG: i.e. the brother of one slain.
173 SM: i.e. fear of retaliation acts as a powerful deterrent for the oppressors.

The reward but of those who war against God and His messenger, and strive to work corruption in the land, that they be killed, or they be crucified, or their hands and feet be cut off on opposite sides, or they be banished from the land.[174] That[...]. They have disgrace in the World; and they have in the Hereafter a great punishment
(5:33)

We sent down the Torah wherein is guidance and light. The prophets who submitted judged thereby those who hold to Judaism as did the rabbis and the religious scholars with what they were given charge of the Writ of God and were thereto witnesses: "So fear not mankind but fear Me; and sell not My proofs at a cheap price." And whoso judges not by what God has sent down, it is they who are the false claimers of guidance.

And We prescribed for them therein a life for a life, and an eye for an eye, and a nose for a nose, and an ear for an ear, and a tooth for a tooth, and for wounds just requital; but whoso forgives it by way of charity, it is an expiation for him. And whoso judges not by what God has sent down: it is they who are the wrongdoers.
(5:44-45)

Do not kill unjustly

O you who heed warning: consume not your wealth among yourselves in vanity, or save by way of trade by mutual consent among you; and kill not yourselves;[175] God is merciful to you;
(4:29)

---

174 SM: These punishments are in are in line with just requital i.e. tyrants who commit atrocities such as crucifixion, killing or cutting off the hands and feet on opposite sides must be punished with like punishment. See examples of such acts committed by an archetypal tyrant (Pharoah) in 7:124 and 7:127.

175 SM: Arberry translates as *And kill not one another*.

For that cause We prescribed for the children of Israel that whoso takes a life other than for a life or corruption in the land, it will be as if he killed mankind altogether; (and whoso gives life, it will be as if he gave life to mankind altogether — and Our messengers came to them with clear signs, then many of them after that are committers of excess in the earth —)
(5:32)

And kill not the soul which God has made unlawful save with justice; and whoso is killed wrongfully, We have given authority to his ally; but let him not commit excess in killing; he is supported.
(17:33)

And who call not, with God, to another god, nor kill the soul which God has made unlawful save with justice, nor commit unlawful sexual intercourse;[176] (and whoso does that will meet with a penalty,
(25:68)

Do not kill a believer

It is not for a believer to kill a believer save in error; and whoso kills a believer in error: the manumission of a believing slave, and blood-money delivered to his family save if they forgive by way of charity. And if he[177] be of a people at enmity with you and a believer: the manumission of a believing slave; and if he be of a people between whom and you is a treaty: blood-money delivered to his family, and the manumission of a believing slave. And whoso has not the means: a fast of two months consecutively as repentance from God; and God is knowing and wise.

---

176 SG: The root (z-n-y) conveys senses of *unlawful sexual intercourse* (sexual congress between two people who are not married to each other) and occurs at 17:32, 24:2, 24:2, 24:3, 24:3, 24:3, 24:3, 25:68, 60:12.
177 SG: i.e. the deceased.

And whoso kills a believer intentionally: his reward is Gehenna, he abiding eternally therein; and God is wroth with him, and has cursed him, and has prepared for him a great punishment.
(4:92-93)

Fight in the cause of God

God sanctions a war against aggressors and oppressors only. The below verses are particularly instructive in this regard.[178]

Hast thou not considered those who went forth from their habitations in their thousands, fearing death? And God said to them: "Die"; then gave He them life. God is bountiful to mankind, but most men are not grateful.
And fight in the cause of God, and know that God is hearing and knowing.
Who is it that will lend to God a goodly loan that He might multiply it by many multiples for him? And God constricts and expands; and to Him will you be returned.
Hast thou not considered the eminent ones of the children of Israel after Moses? When they said to a prophet of theirs: "Raise thou up for us a king; we will fight in the cause of God," he said: "Would you, if fighting be prescribed for you, not fight?" **They said: "And why should we not fight in the cause of God when we have been turned out of our homes, and our children?"** But when fighting was prescribed for them, they turned away save a few of them. And God knows the wrongdoers.
(2:243-246)

And let fight in the cause of God those who sell the life of this world for the Hereafter; and whoso fights in the

---

[178] SM: The phrase *in the cause of God* has a military connotation. See the complete of verses where this phrase occurs: 2:154, 2:190, 2:195, 2:218, 2:244, 2:246, 2:261, 2:262, 2:273, 3:13, 3:146, 3:157, 3:167, 3:169, 4:74, 4:75, 4:76, 4:84, 4:89, 4:94, 4:95, 4:100, 5:54, 8:60, 8:72, 8:74, 9:19, 9:20, 9:34, 9:38, 9:41, 9:60, 9:81, 9:111, 9:120, 16:41, 22:58, 24:22, 47:4, 47:38, 49:15, 57:10, 61:11, 73:20.

> cause of God, be he killed or victorious, We will bestow upon him a great reward.
> **And why should you not fight in the cause of God, and of the oppressed among the men, and the women, and the children who say: "Our Lord: take Thou us out of this city whose people are wrongdoers;** and give Thou us from Thyself an ally; and give Thou us from Thyself a helper"?
> (4:74-75)

God is very clear: there is no compulsion in doctrine.[179] Warmongers will never cease to find creative ways to twist God's imperatives to justify "holy" wars but the fact of the matter is that *fighting in the cause of God* is only ordained when an aggressor attacks you or oppresses a people.

> And fight in the cause of God those who fight you,[180] but transgress not; God loves not the transgressors.
> And kill them wheresoever you find them,[181] and turn them out from wheresoever they turned you out; and means of denial[182] is worse than killing. And fight them not in the inviolable place of worship until they fight you therein. But if they fight you, then kill them; thus is the reward of the false claimers of guidance.
> But if they desist, then God is forgiving and merciful.
> And fight them until there is no more means of denial[183] and the doctrine belongs to God;[184] but if they desist, then is there no enmity save against the wrongdoers.

---

179 SM: "There is no compulsion in doctrine; sound judgment has become clear from error. So whoso denies idols and believes in God, he has grasped the most firm handhold which has no break; and God is hearing and knowing." (2:256)
180 SG: In terms of strategy, a defensive war is not only morally superior, it is typically the most efficient and effective.
181 SG: i.e. those who have elected to fight you.
182 SM: Arberry translates as *persecution*.
183 SM: Arberry translates as *persecution*. SG: Arabic: *dīn*. See Notepad V; i.e. your doctrine. Such war is sanctioned only when outsiders choose to impose their faith — or lack thereof — upon the believers. We have no business imposing our faith on them. We are to warn them, then leave them to God. But if they attack us, we are to defend ourselves.
184 SM: "There is no compulsion in doctrine.." (See 2:256) is in itself part of God's doctrine. The salient point is that we must not impose our faith on others. We are permitted only

The inviolable month is for the inviolable month, and the inviolable deeds are just requital: whoso transgressed against you, transgress against him just as he transgressed against you. But be in prudent fear of God, and know that God is with those of prudent fear.

And spend in the cause of God, and give not yourselves over to destruction. And do good; God loves the doers of good.

(2:190-195)

Those who heed warning fight in the cause of God; and those who ignore warning fight in the cause of idols. Then fight the allies of the satan; the plan of the satan is weak.

Hast thou not considered those to whom it was said: "Restrain your hands;[185] and uphold the duty, and render the purity," but when fighting is prescribed for them, then a faction among them fears men like the fear of God, or a stronger fear? And they said: "Our Lord: why hast Thou prescribed fighting for us? Oh, that Thou wouldst but delay us a little while!" Say thou: "Little is the enjoyment of the World"; and the Hereafter is better for him who is in prudent fear; and you will not be wronged a hair upon a date-stone.

(4:76-77)

So fight thou in the cause of God; thou art not charged save with thyself. And rouse thou the believers: it may be that God will restrain the might of those who ignore warning; and God is stronger in might, and stronger in exemplary punishment.

(4:84)

Those who ignore warning spend their wealth on turning away from the path of God. So will they spend it; then

---

to fight the oppressors and aggressors. (See 2:190, 2:246, 4:75).
185 SM: i.e. they were warned to not spread corruption in the land.

will it become a sorrow for them; then will they be defeated, and those who ignore warning will be gathered into Gehenna,

That God might separate the bad from the good. And the bad will He place one upon another, and heap it all together, and place it in Gehenna; it is they who are the losers.

Say thou to those who ignore warning: if they cease, what is past will be forgiven them; but if they return, then the practice of the former peoples has gone before.

And fight them until there is no means of denial,[186] and the doctrine is entirely for God;[187] and if they cease, God sees what they do.

(8:36-39)

What is in the heavens and what is in the earth gives glory to God; and He is the Exalted in Might, the Wise.

O you who heed warning: why do you say what you do not?

Great is the hatred in the sight of God, that you say what you do not.

God loves those who fight in His cause in ranks, as though they were a compacted structure.

(61:1-4)

I have left out commands related to fighting in the cause of God in Chapter 9 of the Qur'an because the whole chapter deals with a specific event (the breaking of a treaty between the believers and the idolaters) during the time of the Messenger. A fuller study of this chapter to derive additional rules of war can be done if the need arises.

Fighting prohibited during four out of twelve lunar months

God has decreed four months[188] out of a span of twelve lunar months

---

186 SM: See my note in 2:143 above.
187 SM: See my note in 2:143 above.
188 SM: Lunar months.

to be inviolable i.e. fighting is prohibited in them.[189] Since the Qur'an does not give us information as to which months these are, it leads me to believe that it is left up to the believers to decide which four lunar months out of a twelve month lunar span to make inviolable. A working example of how this was done during the time of the Messenger is provided below.

> An acquittal from God and His messenger, to those with whom you made a covenant among the idolaters:
> "Travel in the earth four months;[190] and know that you cannot escape God, and that God will disgrace the false claimers of guidance."
> And a proclamation from God and His messenger to mankind on the day of the greater pilgrimage: "God is free of the idolaters, as is His messenger. And if you repent, it is better for you; but if you turn away, know that you cannot escape God." And bear thou tidings to those who ignore warning of a painful punishment,
> Save the idolaters with whom you made a covenant then who have not been deficient towards you in anything, nor assisted anyone against you; so fulfil to them your covenant to its term; God loves those of prudent fear.
> And when the inviolable months have passed,[191] then kill the idolaters wheresoever you find them, and seize them, and restrain them, and lie in wait for them at every place of ambush. But if they repent, and uphold the duty, and render the purity, then let them go their way; God is forgiving and merciful.
> (9:1-5)

In a span of twelve lunar months, four lunar months must be considered inviolable.[192] Postponement is not allowed i.e. we cannot make

---

189 See 9:36-37.
190 SM: The four lunar months at the time of this proclamation would then be considered inviolable.
191 SM: The four lunar months which were made inviolable at the time of the proclamation. See 9:2.
192 SM: Some Qur'anic commentators think that God is condemning the practice of

two lunar months inviolable in a twelve lunar month span and then "catch-up" by making six months inviolable in the next span.

> The count of months is with God; twelve months were in the Writ of God the day He created the heavens and the earth; from it are four inviolable. That is the right doctrine, so wrong not your souls concerning them: — and fight the idolaters altogether as they fight you altogether, and know that God is with those of prudent fear —
> Postponement is but an increase in denial whereby those who ignore warning are led astray; they make it lawful one year and make it unlawful another year, that the count might agree with what God made unlawful — so they make lawful what God made unlawful; made fair to them is the evil of their deeds; and God guides not the people of the false claimers of guidance.
> (9:36-37)

> Fighting is prescribed for you, though it be hateful to you. And it may be that you hate a thing and it is good for you; and it may be that you love a thing and it is bad for you. And God knows, and you know not.
> They ask thee about the inviolable month,[193] fighting therein; say thou: "Fighting therein is grave, but turning away from the path of God, and denial of Him and the inviolable place of worship, and the expulsion of its people therefrom is graver in the sight of God; and means of denial[194] is worse than killing." And they will not cease to fight you until they turn you from your doctrine, if they are able; and whoso among you turns from

---

intercalation (adding an extra month every few years to bring the lunar calendar back in sync with the seasons). I, however, think that God is simply stating that He created a time-span unit (which we call a year) to be the duration of twelve lunar months and out of these four are inviolable. See https://theos-sphragis.info/hebrew_babylonian_intercalation.html for more information on intercalation.
193 SG: Arabic: *al shahr al ḥarām*. See note to 2:194; i.e. at such time as fighting is forbidden (by convention or treaty).
194 SM: Arberry translates as: *persecution*.

his doctrine, and dies a false claimer of guidance: those, their works are vain in the World and in the Hereafter; and those are the companions of the Fire; therein they abide eternally.

Those who heed warning, and those who emigrate and strive in the cause of God: those hope for the mercy of God; and God is forgiving and merciful.

(2:216-218)

Verify intelligence before you act

O you who heed warning: when you go forth in the cause of God, verify; and say not to one who offers you peace: "Thou art not a believer," seeking the transitory things of the life of this world; for with God are many spoils. Thus were you before, but God was gracious to you. So verify; God is aware of what you do.

(4:94)

O you who heed warning: if one perfidious comes to you with a report: verify, lest you strike a people in ignorance, and become remorseful for what you did.

And know that among you is the messenger of God. If he were to obey you in much of the matter, you would be distressed. But God has endeared to you faith, and made it fair in your hearts, and has made hateful to you denial and perfidy and opposition — it is they who are the right-minded —

As bounty and favour from God; and God is knowing and wise.

(49:6-8)

Do not turn your backs to an enemy in battle unless...

O you who heed warning: when you meet those who ignore warning advancing, turn not your backs to them.
And whoso, that day, turns his back to them save as a manoeuvre for battle, or joining a company, he has incurred wrath from God; and his shelter is Gehenna; and evil is the journey's end.
(8:15-16)

Make right between believers but fight the oppressor

And if two groups of the believers fight: make right between them; and if one of them oppress the other: fight that which oppresses until it returns to the command of God. And if it returns, then make right between them with justice; and be equitable; God loves the equitable.
The believers are brethren, so make right between your two brothers; and be in prudent fear of God, that you might obtain mercy.
(49:9-10)

Do not sorrow for those killed in the cause of God

O you who heed warning: be not like those who ignore warning, and say of their brothers when they travel in the earth or are on an expedition: "Had they been with us, they would not have died or been killed," that God might make that a sorrow in their hearts; for God gives life, and gives death; and God sees what you do.
And if you are killed or die in the cause of God, pardon from God and mercy are better than what they amass.
And if you die or are killed, to God will you be gathered.
And think not of those who are killed in the cause of God as dead; nay, they are alive, with their Lord receiving provision,
Exulting in what God has bestowed upon them of His bounty; and rejoicing in those behind them who are

>   yet to join them, that no fear will be upon them, nor will they grieve;
> Rejoicing in favour and bounty from God, and that God causes not to be lost the reward of the believers.
>
> (3:156-171)

This chapter should lay to rest the false Western notion that the Writ of God sanctions the killing of infidels. God commands us to fight only in the case of self-defense or to defend the oppressed in the land. It does not sanction a war otherwise, no matter how noble the given cause may be.

We shall now look at the subject of charity in the Writ of God.

9
CHARITY

Then as for the fatherless: oppress thou not.
And as for the petitioner: repel thou not.
(93:9-10)

Spend of what God has provided you

alif lām mīm
That is the Writ about which there is no doubt, a guidance to those of prudent fear:
Those who believe in the Unseen, and uphold the duty, and of what We have provided them they spend;
(2:1-3)

O you who heed warning: spend of what We have provided you before there comes a day wherein is neither commerce, nor friendship, nor intercession; and the false claimers of guidance: they are the wrongdoers.
(2:254)

Those who say: "Our Lord: we believe, so forgive Thou us our transgressions, and protect Thou us from the punishment of the Fire,"
The patient, the truthful, the humbly obedient, those who spend, and the seekers of forgiveness at dawn. (3:16-17)

The believers are but those who when God is remembered, their hearts are afraid, and when His proofs are recited to them, it increases them in faith, and in their Lord they place their trust,

Those who uphold the duty, and of what We have provided them they spend:

(8:2-3)

Those who fulfil the covenant of God, and break not the agreement,

And who join what God commanded to be joined, and fear their Lord, and dread the evil of the reckoning,

And who are patient seeking the face of their Lord, and uphold the duty, and spend of what We have provided them, secretly and openly, and they avert evil with good: those have the good final abode:

(13:20-22)

Say thou to My servants who heed warning, that they uphold the duty, and spend of what We have provided them, secretly and openly, before there comes a day wherein there is neither bargaining nor friendship.

(14:31)

And for every community We appointed a rite: that they remember the name of God over what He has provided them of livestock cattle. And your God is One God; so submit to Him. And bear thou glad tidings to the humble:

Whose hearts are afraid when God is remembered, and those patient over what befalls them, and who uphold the duty, and of what We have provided them they spend.

(22:34-35)

Those to whom We gave the Writ before it, they believe in it,

And when it is recited to them, they say: "We believe in it. It is the truth from our Lord; before it were we submitting."

Those will be given their reward twice over because they were patient. And they avert evil with good, and of what We have provided them they spend;
(28:52-54)

Only those believe in Our proofs who, when they are reminded thereof, fall down in submission; and they give glory with the praise of their Lord, and they wax not proud.
Their sides forsake their beds; they call to their Lord in fear and hope, and of what We have provided them they spend.
(32:15-16)

Say thou: "My Lord expands provision for whom He wills of His servants, and He straitens for him." And what you have spent of anything, He will replace it; and He is the best of providers.
(34:39)

Those who recite the Writ of God and uphold the duty and spend of what We have provided them, secretly and openly, expect a trade that perishes not,
That He will pay their rewards in full, and increase them out of His bounty; He is forgiving and appreciative.
(35:29-30)

And when it is said to them: "Spend of what God has provided you," those who ignore warning say to those who heed warning: "Shall we feed one whom, had God willed, He would have fed? You are only in manifest error."
(36:47)

And those who respond to their Lord, and uphold the duty, and their affair is by consultation between them, and of what We have provided them they spend.
(42:38)

> Believe in God and His messenger, and spend of that whereof He has made you heirs. And those who heed warning among you and spend: theirs will be a great reward.
> (57:7)

> O you who heed warning: let not your wealth or your children divert you from the remembrance of God; and whoso does that, it is they who are the losers.
> And spend of what We have provided you before death comes to one among you and he says: "My Lord: hadst Thou but delayed me to a near term, that I might give charity and be among the righteous!"
> But God delays no soul when its term comes; and God is aware of what you do.
> (63:9-11)

> So be in prudent fear of God as much as you are able, and listen, and obey, and spend; it is better for your souls. And whoso is protected from the avarice of his soul, it is they who are the successful.
> (64:16)

Spend in the cause of God

Spending in the cause of God means to contribute money towards fighting *in the cause of God*. As mentioned in the previous chapter, fighting in the cause of God is only sanctioned against aggressors and oppressors.

> And fight in the cause of God those who fight you,[195] but transgress not; God loves not the transgressors.
> And kill them wheresoever you find them,[196] and turn them out from wheresoever they turned you out; and

---

[195] SG: In terms of strategy, a defensive war is not only morally superior, it is typically the most efficient and effective.
[196] SG: I.e. those who have elected to fight you.

means of denial[197] is worse than killing. And fight them not in the inviolable place of worship until they fight you therein. But if they fight you, then kill them; thus is the reward of the false claimers of guidance.

But if they desist, then God is forgiving and merciful.

And fight them until there is no more means of denial[198] and the doctrine belongs to God;[199] but if they desist, then is there no enmity save against the wrongdoers.

The inviolable month is for the inviolable month, and the inviolable deeds are just requital: whoso transgressed against you, transgress against him just as he transgressed against you. But be in prudent fear of God, and know that God is with those of prudent fear.

And spend in the cause of God, and give not yourselves over to destruction. And do good; God loves the doers of good.

(2:190-195)

The likeness of those who spend their wealth in the cause of God is as the likeness of a grain which grows seven ears, in each ear a hundred grains. And God increases manifold to whom He wills; and God is encompassing and knowing.

Those who spend their wealth in the cause of God, then follow not what they have spent with condescension or hindrance, they have their reward with their Lord; and no fear will be upon them, nor will they grieve.

Fitting speech and blindness to deficiency[200] are better than charity followed by hindrance; and God is free from need and clement.

---

197 SM: Arberry translates as persecution.
198 SM: Arberry translates as *persecution*. SG: Arabic: *dīn*. See Notepad V; i.e. your doctrine. Such war is sanctioned only when outsiders choose to impose their faith — or lack thereof — upon the believers. We have no business imposing our faith on them. We are to warn them, then leave them to God. But if they attack us, we are to defend ourselves.
199 SM: "There is no compulsion in doctrine.." (See 2:256) is in itself part of God's doctrine. The salient point is that we must not impose our faith on others. We are permitted only to fight the aggressors and oppressors. (See 2:190, 2:246, 4:75).
200 SM: I agree with Arberry's rendering "Honourable words, and forgiveness".

O you who heed warning: make not your charity vain through condescension and hindrance, like one who spends his wealth to be seen of men and believes not in God and the Last Day. And his likeness is as the likeness of a rock whereon is dust: a downpour fell upon it leaving it bare; they possess nothing from what they have earned; and God guides not the people of the false claimers of guidance.

And the likeness of those who spend their wealth seeking the pleasure of God and as a confirmation[201] of their souls,[202] is as the likeness of a garden on high ground: a downpour fell upon it, and it yielded double fruit; and if a downpour falls not upon it, then fine rain; and God sees what you do.

Would one of you wish to have a garden of date-palms and grapevines, beneath which rivers flow, he having every fruit therein?[...]. And old age befell him, and he had weak progeny, and a cyclone wherein was fire befell it, and it was burned up. Thus does God make plain to you the proofs, that you might give thought.
(2:261-266)

And let not those who ignore warning think they have got away; they cannot escape.

And prepare for them what you are able of forces and of cavalry, to terrify thereby the enemy of God, and your enemy, and others besides them whom you know not; God knows them. And whatever you spend in the cause of God will be repaid to you in full; and you will not be wronged.

And if they incline to peace, then incline thou to it; and place thou thy trust in God; He is the Hearing, the Knowing.
(8:59-61)

---

201 SG: Arabic: *tathbīt* — confirmation; strengthening; corroboration, substantiation.
202 SG: i.e. to prove their faith by deeds.

And what is with you that you spend not in the cause of God, when to God belongs the inheritance of the heavens and the earth? Not equal among you is he who spent and who fought before the victory — those are greater in degree than those who spent and fought afterwards. But to each has God promised the best; and God is aware of what you do.
(57:10)

Spend of the good and not the bad

O you who heed warning: spend of the good things you have earned, and of what We have brought forth for you from the earth. And resort not to the bad thereof, to spend thereof, when you would not take it save you closed an eye to it; and know that God is free from need and praiseworthy.

The satan promises you poverty, and enjoins upon you sexual immorality, but God promises you forgiveness and bounty from Him; and God is encompassing and knowing.

He gives wisdom to whom He wills; and to whom wisdom is given, he has been given much good; but only those of insight take heed.

And what you spend of an expenditure or make of a pledge, God knows it. And there are for the wrongdoers no helpers.

If you reveal charity, excellent is it; but if you hide it, and give it to the poor, it is better for you, and He will remove from you some of your evil deeds; and God is aware of what you do.

(Not upon thee is their guidance; but God guides whom He wills.) And what you spend of good, it is for yourselves. And spend not save seeking the face of God (and what you spend of good will be paid in full to you; and you will not be wronged)

On the poor who are straitened in the cause of God, unable to make a way in the earth: the ignorant considers them free from need due to their reticence. Thou wilt know them by their mark: they do not ask of men importunately. And what you spend of good, God knows it.

Those who spend their wealth by night and by day, secretly and openly: they have their reward with their Lord; and no fear will be upon them, nor will they grieve.
(2:267-274)

You attain not to virtue until you spend of what you love; and what you spend of anything, God knows it.
(3:92)

Spend on your parents, relatives, the fatherless, the needy and those engaged in the cause of God

They ask thee what they should spend. Say thou: "Whatever you spend of good for parents and relatives, and the fatherless, and the needy, and the wayfarer,[...]. And whatever you do of good, God knows it."
(2:215)

Spend in prosperity and in adversity

And vie one with another for forgiveness from your Lord, and a garden as wide as the heavens and the earth prepared for those of prudent fear:

Those who spend in prosperity and in adversity, and who control their wrath, and forgive men; and God loves the doers of good;
(3:133-134)

Moderate your charity

And let not those who are miserly with what God gives them of His bounty think it good for them; the truth is, it

is evil for them: hung about their necks will be that with which they were miserly on the Day of Resurrection; and to God belongs the inheritance of the heavens and the earth; and God is aware of what you do.
(3:180)

And serve God, and ascribe not a partnership with Him to anything; and towards parents good conduct, and towards relatives, and the fatherless, and the poor, and the neighbour who is kin, and the neighbour who is not kin, and the companion at your side, and the wayfarer, and those whom your right hands possess; God loves not whoso is a conceited boaster:
Those who are miserly and enjoin miserliness upon men, and conceal what God has bestowed upon them of His bounty; and We have prepared for the false claimers of guidance a humiliating punishment;
And those who spend their wealth to be seen of men, and believe not in God or the Last Day; and to whom the satan is a companion, then evil is he as a companion.
And how would it harm them if they believed in God and the Last Day, and spent of what God has provided them? And God is of them knowing.
(4:36-39)

And the servants of the Almighty are they who walk upon the earth modestly, and when the ignorant address them, they speak peace;
And who spend the night to their Lord submitting and standing;
(25:63-64)

And who, when they spend, are neither extravagant nor miserly; — and there is a place in-between —
(25:67)

And give thou the relative his due, and the needy, and the
wayfarer; but squander thou not wastefully,
The squanderers are brothers of the satans, and the satan
is to his Lord ungrateful.
(17:26-27)

God does not accept from the perfidious

Say thou: "Do you await for us save one of the two best
things? And we await for you, that God will afflict you
with a punishment from Him or at our hands. So wait
— we are with you waiting."
Say thou: "Spend willingly or unwillingly, it will not be
accepted from you; you are perfidious[203] people."
And there prevents their expenditures being accepted
from them only that they denied God and His messenger,
and come not to the duty save as idlers, and spend not
save unwillingly.
(9:52-54)

Spend only seeking God's approval

And among the desert Arabs is he who believes in God
and the Last Day, and takes what he spends as a means
of nearness to God and the duties of the Messenger. In
truth, it is a means of nearness for them: God will make
them enter into His mercy; God is forgiving and merciful.
(9:99)

So give thou the relative his due, and the needy, and the
wayfarer. That is best for those who desire the face of
God; and it is they who are the successful.
(30:38)

---

203 SM: See the following verses where this word is used to gain a better understanding of what God means by the perfidious people: 2:26, 2:99, 3:82, 3:110, 5:25, 5:26, 5:47, 5:49, 5:59, 5:81, 5:108, 7:102, 7:145, 9:8, 9:24, 9:53, 9:67, 9:80, 9:84, 9:96, 21:74, 24:4, 24:55, 27:12, 28:32, 32:18, 43:54, 46:35, 49:6, 51:46, 57:16, 57:26, 57:27, 59:5, 59:19, 61:5, 63:6.

We shall now look at what the Writ of God has to say about sexual immorality; a disease which has spread far and wide in today's age.

10
SEXUAL IMMORALITY

The satan promises you poverty, and enjoins upon you sexual immorality, but God promises you forgiveness and bounty from Him; and God is encompassing and knowing.
(2:268)

There are three types of sexual immorality[204] mentioned in the God's Writ:[205] marrying the wife of one's father, approaching the same gender with lust and having sexual intercourse outside of wedlock.

And marry not what your fathers married[206] among women save what is past; **it was sexual immorality,** and hateful, and an evil path.
(4:22)

---

204 SM: Arabic: *fahsha* (singular), *fahishat* (plural)
205 SM: I give credit to Brother Gerrans for this insight and refer the interested reader to Notepad XI.iii (Page 34) of "Addenda to The Qur'an: A Complete Revelation": https://quranite.com/wp-content/uploads/Addenda-to-The-Quran-A-Complete-Revelation.pdf
206 SG: I take this to close the door to two sins at once: the sin of sexual relations with a previous wife of one's father, and any attempt to increase one's share of one's father's estate by marrying his widow.

And Lot: when he said to his people: "**Do you commit sexual immorality,** that none among all mankind has preceded you?
"**You approach men with lust rather than women;** the truth is, you are a people committing excess."
(7:80-81)

And Lot: when he said to his people: "**Do you commit sexual immorality with open eyes?**
"**Do you approach men with lust instead of women?** The truth is, you are a people in ignorance."
(27:54-55)

And she in whose house he was sought to lure him away from his soul;[207] and she closed the doors, **and said: "Come thou hither."** He said: "I seek refuge in God — He is my Lord who made good my dwelling; the wrongdoers do not succeed."
And she desired him; and he desired her[...] were it not that he saw the evidence of his Lord. Thus — that We might turn away from him **evil and sexual immorality;** he was among Our sincere servants.
(12:23-24)

And approach not unlawful sexual intercourse[208] — it is sexual immorality, and evil as a path —
(17:32)

Prohibition on sexual immorality

And when they commit sexual immorality, they say: "We found our fathers doing it," and: "God enjoined it upon us." Say thou: "God enjoins not sexual immorality; do you ascribe to God what you know not?" (7:28)

---

207 SG: i.e. to seduce him.
208 SG: The root (z-n-y) conveys senses of *unlawful sexual intercourse* (sexual congress between two people who are not married to each other) and occurs at 17:32, 24:2, 24:2, 24:3, 24:3, 24:3, 24:3, 25:68, 60:12.

> Say thou: "My Lord has only made unlawful sexual immoralities — whether open or concealed — and sin, and sectarian zealotry without cause, and that you ascribe a partnership with God to that for which He has not sent down authority, and that you ascribe to God what you know not."
> (7:33)

Punishment for sexual intercourse outside of wedlock

It goes without saying that the punishment for sexual intercourse outside of wedlock is applicable only in a believing community i.e. a community that is implementing God's Writ. Only a fool would use these verses to mete out vigilante justice in a secular society.[209]

> A *sūrah* We have sent down and made obligatory, and wherein We sent down clear proofs, that you might take heed:
> The unchaste woman[210] and the unchaste man: lash each one of the two[211] with a hundred lashes,[212] and let not pity for them take you concerning the doctrine of God if you believe in God and the Last Day. And let witness their punishment a number of the believers.

---

209 SM: which, unfortunately, is the dominant society of the world at the moment.
210 SG: The root (*z-n-y*) conveys senses of *unlawful sexual intercourse* (sexual congress between two people who are not married to each other) and occurs at 17:32, 24:2, 24:2, 24:3, 24:3, 24:3, 24:3, 25:68, 60:12.
211 SG: Grammar: dual. The grammar itself makes clear that such people are both to be punished. In those countries called Islamic, this stipulation is routinely ignored, even in those rare cases where the witness requirement and punishment is as found in the Qur'an. All too often a woman is punished alone, a practice which falls directly foul of this verse.
212 SG: The Traditionalist claims that this applies only to those who are not unmarried and that in cases where the people are married (to other people) the punishment is stoning to death. He can point to no Qur'anic justification for this. The Qur'anic punishment is clear, and administrable only where there are four reliable witnesses to the fact. Stoning or other forms of capital punishment against fornicators of any kind constitute crimes for which the perpetrators will have to answer to God.

The unchaste man²¹³ shall not marry save an unchaste woman or an idolatress; and an unchaste woman shall not marry save an unchaste man or an idolater — and that is unlawful to the believers —

And those who accuse chaste women then bring not four witnesses:²¹⁴ lash them with eighty lashes, and accept not of them witness ever — and it is they who are the perfidious —

Save those who repent after that and make right; then is God forgiving and merciful.

And those who accuse their wives and have no witnesses save themselves, then the witness of one of them is four witnesses by God that he is of the truthful,

And the fifth, that the curse of God be upon him if he is of the liars.

And it averts the punishment from her that she bear witness: four witnesses by God that he is of the liars,

And the fifth, that the wrath of God be upon her if he is of the truthful.

(24:1-9)

Punishment for approaching the same gender with lust

While most translators consider the below verses a prescription for sexual intercourse between a man and a woman outside of wedlock, God has already given us a punishment for that offense in 24:2. In my view, the below verses are a punishment for the sexual immorality of approaching the same gender with lust. Women guilty of approaching the same sex with lust must be put under house-arrest and men guilty of approaching the same sex with lust must be hindered.

---

213 SG: The root (z-n-y) conveys senses of *unlawful sexual intercourse* (sexual congress between two people who are not married to each other) and occurs at 17:32, 24:2, 24:2, 24:3, 24:3, 24:3, 24:3, 25:68, 60:12.

214 SG: A witness is someone who has personally seen an event; there is no other kind.

> And those who commit sexual immorality[215] among your women, call to witness against them four from among you; then if they bear witness, confine them to houses[216] until death takes them, or God makes for them another path.
> And the two[217] who commit it among you, hinder them; but if they repent and make right, let them be; God is accepting of repentance and merciful.
> (4:15-16)

Sadly, moderns have no idea of the importance of the preservation of one's chastity in the doctrine of God. Sexual immorality destroys men, destroys families and ultimately, society itself.

We shall now look at the subject of modesty in God's Writ which ties in closely with the discussion above.

---

215 SG: While this is translated variously by the Traditionalist, we do not have to guess as to the meaning. The Qur'an applies *fāḥish* (sg.) to three scenarios only: sex outside of marriage (17:32); marrying the wife of one's father (4:22); and male homosexuality (7:80- 81, 27:54-55).
216 SM: i.e. house-arrest.
217 SM: i.e. two men. Grammar is masculine dual. Abdel Haleem translates as "if two men".

11
MODESTY

O children of Adam: let not the satan subject you to means of denial as he turned your parents out of the garden, removing from them their raiment, that he might make manifest their shame to them. He and his kind see you from where you see them not. We have made the satans allies of those who do not believe.
(7:27)

Keep away from your wives during menstruation

And they ask thee about menstruation. Say thou: "It is a hindrance; so keep away from women during menstruation, and approach them not until they are clean. And when they have purified themselves, then approach them in what manner God has commanded you;[218] God loves those who repent and loves those who purify themselves. "Your women are a tilth for you; so come to your tilth as you will, and send ahead for your souls; and be in prudent fear of God, and know that you will meet Him." And bear thou glad tidings to the believers.
(2:222-223)

Hide your shame

---

218 SM: The command follows in the next verse.

O children of Adam: We have sent down upon you raiment to hide your shame,[219] and as adornment; but the raiment of prudent fear, that is best. That is among the proofs of God, that they might take heed.

O children of Adam: let not the satan subject you to means of denial as he turned your parents out of the garden, removing from them their raiment, that he might make manifest their shame to them. He and his kind see you from where you see them not. We have made the satans allies of those who do not believe.

And when they commit sexual immorality, they say: "We found our fathers doing it," and: "God enjoined it upon us." Say thou: "God enjoins not sexual immorality; do you ascribe to God what you know not?"

Say thou: "My Lord has enjoined equity. Uphold your countenances[220] at every place of worship, and call to Him, sincere to Him in doctrine; as He created you, so you will return."

A faction He guided, and upon a faction was misguidance due: they took the satans as allies instead of God, and think they are guided.

O children of Adam: take your adornment[221] at every place of worship; and eat and drink, but commit not excess; God loves not the committers of excess.

Say thou: "Who has made unlawful the adornment of God which He brought forth for His servants, and the good things of provision?" Say thou: "These are for those who heed warning in the life of this world exclusively on the

---

219 SG: i.e. private parts.
220 SG: Arabic: *wajh — face, countenance, personality, true self.* I take the collocation to uphold one's countenance to mean to (be able to) hold one's head up high in English. The preceding context is the key: by staying sexually clean, observing equity (which means integrity and consistency with inner convictions on the one hand, and faith in God alone on the other — see 3:18 and note thereto) one may come before God in prayer and worship in an effective manner. Without sexual purity, it is not possible. This is why all Satanic systems promote illicit sex as virtue.
221 SM: See these verses to gain a better idea of what adornment means: 7:31, 7:32, 10:88, 11:15, 16:8, 18:7, 18:28, 18:46, 20:59, 20:87, 24:31, 24:60, 28:60, 28:79, 33:28, 37:6, 57:20.

Day of Resurrection." Thus do We set out and detail the proofs for people who know.
(7:26-32)

Lower your sight and dress modestly

Say thou to the believing men that they lower some of their sight, and preserve their chastity;[222] that is purer for them. God is aware of what they do.

And say thou to the believing women, that they lower some of their sight, and preserve their chastity,[223] and that they show not their adornment[224] save that apparent of it, and that they draw their coverings over their bosoms and not reveal their adornment save to their husbands, or their fathers, or the fathers of their husbands, or their sons, or the sons of their husbands, or their brothers, or the sons of their brothers, or the sons of their sisters, or their women, or what their right hands possess, or male attendants who have not the resourcefulness of men,[225] or the children not yet aware of a woman's private parts. And let them not strike their feet to make known what they hide of their adornment.[226] And turn to God altogether, O believers, that you might be successful.
(24:30-31)

While the above is used to justify the Islamic head and face covering,[227] a careful reading yields the following points:

1. Believing men and women must lower their eyes and preserve their chastity i.e. guard their private parts
2. Believing women should cover their bosoms[228]

---
222 SM: Arberry translates as *guard their private parts*.
223 SM: Arberry translates as *guard their private parts*.
224 SM: See these verses to gain a better idea of what adornment means: 7:31, 7:32, 10:88, 11:15, 16:8, 18:7, 18:28, 18:46, 20:59, 20:87, 24:31, 24:60, 28:60, 28:79, 33:28, 37:6, 57:20.
225 SM: Arberry translates as *not having sexual desire*.
226 SM: They should not walk in this manner as it will draw male attention to them.
227 SM: *Hijab* and *niqab* respectively.
228 SM: Lane's lexicon states *the opening of a shirt at the uppermost part of the breast*. In

3. Believing women should not reveal their adornment[229] except to their husbands, or their fathers, or the fathers of their husbands, or their sons, or the sons of their husbands, or their brothers, or the sons of their brothers, or the sons of their sisters, or their women, or what their right hands possess, or male attendants who have not the resourcefulness of men, or the children not yet aware of a woman's private parts
4. Believing women should not strike their feet to make known what they hide of their adornment i.e. they are not to walk in a sexually provocative manner

The incessant nit-picking of God's commands in 24:31-32 by Muslims is, unfortunately, a symptom of a disease in their hearts.[230] Muslims routinely ignore major and clear portions of God's Writ while quibbling over commands which God has left ambiguous. The reason for the ambiguity present in 24:31-32 is to allow for flexibility in their implementation in different societies and times.

In any case, a believing woman would do well to work on purifying her heart and being genuinely modest; God knows what is in the hearts.

The command to draw down garments

> Those who hinder God and His messenger: God has cursed them in the World and the Hereafter, and has prepared for them a humiliating punishment.
> And those who hinder believing men and believing women with what they have not earned: they bear a calumny and obvious sin.

---

modern parlance, we could say *to cover your cleavage*.

229 SM: A pan-textual analysis of this word is instructive: 7:31, 7:32, 10:88, 11:15, 16:8, 18:7, 18:28, 18:46, 20:59, 20:87, 24:31, 24:60, 28:60, 28:79, 33:28, 37:6, 57:20.

230 SM: "He it is that sent down upon thee the Writ; among it are explicit proofs: they are the foundation of the Writ; and others are ambiguous. Then as for those in whose hearts is deviation: they follow what is ambiguous thereof, seeking the means of denial, and seeking its interpretation. And no one knows its interpretation save God, and those firm in knowledge; they say: "We believe in it; all is from our Lord." But only those of insight take heed." (3:7)

> O Prophet: say thou to thy wives, and thy daughters, and the women of the believers, that they draw down[231] over them some of their garments. That will tend to them being recognised and not hindered; and God is forgiving and merciful.
> If the waverers desist not,[232] and those in whose hearts is disease, and the spreaders of lies in the city, We will impel thee against them; then will they not be your neighbours therein save a little,
> Ones cursed: wherever they are found, taken and comprehensively killed.
> The practice of God among those who passed away before[...]; and thou wilt not find for the practice of God any replacement.
> (33:57-62)

Contextual reading (which is imperative in order to understand the commands of God) leaves no doubt that the command for the believing women to draw down over them some of their garments was for the express purpose of being recognized as believing women and left alone by men on that basis. This solution was for the specific problem of the waverers harassing (believing) women (during the time of the Messenger) and using the excuse that they did not recognize them to be believing women.

However, in today's time, the reverse is the case; women who wear the *niqab* and *hijab* are more likely to be harassed due to rampant Islamophobia in the West. A believing woman living in the West would be better served wearing conservative clothing rather than the symbolic Islamic attire as it only serves to attract unwanted attention and enrage the general ignorant public.

Enter houses after asking leave

---

231 SG: i.e. lengthen.
232 SG: In the context, this can reasonably refer only to the harassment of believing women either by direct importunity, or by the spreading of rumours.

O you who heed warning: enter not houses other than your houses until you have asked leave and greeted the people thereof; that is best for you, that you might take heed.

And if you find not therein anyone, then enter not until leave be given you. And if it be said to you: "Go back," then go back; it is purer for you. And God knows what you do.

You do no wrong to enter uninhabited houses in which there is benefit for you. And God knows what you proclaim and what you conceal.
(24:27-29)

Three times of privacy

O you who heed warning: let ask leave of you those whom your right hands possess and those who have not reached puberty[233] among you at three times: before the duty of the dawn, and when you lay aside your garments at noon, and after the duty of the night: three times of nakedness for you; you and they do no wrong beyond them, some of you moving about among others of you. Thus God makes plain to you the proofs; and God is knowing and wise.

And when the children among you reach puberty,[234] then let them ask leave even as those before them asked; thus God makes plain to you His proofs. And God is knowing and wise.

And those past child-bearing among the women who have no hope of marriage: they do no wrong that they lay aside their garments, without displaying adornment; but that they refrain is best for them. And God is hearing and knowing.

No blame is there upon the blind, nor any blame upon the lame, nor any blame upon the sick, nor upon yourselves, that you eat of your houses, or the houses of your

---

233 SM: Minors (not your own children) who might be living in your house.
234 SM: Arberry translates as: *When your children reach puberty.*

fathers, or the houses of your mothers, or the houses of your brothers, or the houses of your sisters, or the houses of your paternal uncles, or the houses of your paternal aunts, or the houses of your maternal uncles, or the houses of your maternal aunts, or that whereof you hold the keys, or of your friend; you do no wrong to eat together or separately. But when you enter houses, greet one another with a greeting from God, blessed and good. Thus God makes plain to you the proofs, that you might use reason.
(24:58-61)

Conservative clothing never goes out of fashion. As we go through this age of insanity, we must always be on our guard against our two enemies: the atheists and the religionists. We should not let their vain desires turn us away from the commands given to us by our Lord and Creator in His Writ.

13
PARTING WORDS

> It is not for a mortal that God should give him the Writ and judgment and prophethood, then he should say to men: "Be servants to me rather than God"; but: **"Be men of God by what you have taught of the Writ, and by what you have studied."**
> (3:79)

I hope this book impresses upon you the importance of understanding and implementing God's Writ in your life. It is *the* key to success for the believers. It is an elegant set of commands; self-consistent and self-referencing, practical and simple. God calls us to serve Him alone. He calls men towards equity, decency and fair-dealing. The only way out of the sorry state of affairs we find ourselves in is by sincerely implementing God's Writ to our utmost strength.

It pains me greatly to see Muslims, who have in their possession the greatest gift bestowed by God upon mankind, failing to implement it. In their monumental arrogance, Muslims have thrown the Writ of God behind their backs in favor of man-made laws. Their stubborn adherence to a religion based primarily on non-Qur'anic literature is the sole cause of their misery. Unless they come back to the Writ of God and implement the commands therein sincerely and exclusively, God will continue to humiliate them in this life and an even greater punishment awaits them in the Hereafter.[235]

---

235 SM: "...Do you believe in part of the Writ and deny part? Then what is the reward of

God in His mercy has guided us, the believers, to the truth. It is now our responsibility to hold fast to God's Writ, and to study and teach it to others.

> And there followed after them successors who inherited the Writ, taking the goods of this fleeting life, and saying: "It will be forgiven us." And if there come to them goods the like thereof, they will take them. **Has there not been taken from them an agreement to the Writ, that they ascribe not to God save the truth, and that they study what is therein?** And the abode of the Hereafter is better for those of prudent fear. Will you then not use reason!
> **And those who hold fast the Writ, and uphold the duty — We cause not to be lost the reward of those who do right.**
> (7:169-170)

***

God causes not to be lost the reward of those who do right. Onwards, O Believers! The Garden awaits.

Your brother in faith,
Said

---

him among you who does that save disgrace in the life of this world? And on the Day of Resurrection they are sent back to the harshest punishment; and God is not unmindful of what you do." (2:85)

OTHER WORKS BY THE AUTHOR

All of my books are available for free at *willyounotreason.com*. Below are the introductions from my other three books: "WillYou Not Reason?", "Tyranny 2.0" and "Cosmology of the Qur'an".

Introduction to Will You Not Reason?

The Qur'an claims to be God's revelation, inspired to the Prophet Muhammad, as a final message for all mankind. Sadly, Muslims, those who most loudly proclaim to hold to the Qur'an, do not understand its message.

I have conducted a sincere and honest study of the Qur'an and have concluded that it can only be from God, the Lord of all creation. The Qur'an is clear, complete, and fully detailed. It warns those who have set up false gods and divided God's doctrine into various religions or sects that they will continue to be humiliated in this life — and severely punished in the Hereafter — unless they repent and turn to the One True God.

In this work, I present God's various arguments for His existence, power, and glory. The creation of the sky and the earth, the sun and the moon, and the male and the female are sufficient proofs of God's benevolence, might and majesty.

The religion of Islam claims to take the Qur'an as foundational scripture but the fact of the matter is that the majority of its doctrinal pillars are not found in the Qur'an. Muslims use the *hadith* — alleged sayings of the Prophet Muhammad — to justify their invented practices when the Qur'an is clear that it alone is *the* source of guidance. Muslims, however, cannot accept this fact because it would involve abandoning the dogma, practices and superstitions of their ancestral religion.

The Qur'an does not contain a blueprint of a religion. God calls all men to believe in Him, the last Day and to serve God alone. God chastises the leaders of all religions of abandoning His scriptures and twisting His words in order to divert men from His straight path.

God promises those who believe in His doctrine and do good works their just rewards in the Hereafter. He calls us to take Him as our only Ally and Protector. He invites all men to carefully consider the Qur'an and to ponder His message carefully. He commands man to use reason — His greatest gift bestowed upon man — to arrive at the true conclusion: that there is one God, without any partners, who created all beings to serve Him alone.

The Qur'an gives us the reality of this life: an exercise in deception, boasting, and competition for increase; it is fragile and fleeting. True life awaits after death. So let us strive for God's acceptance and the attainment of the Garden in the Hereafter; a believer's ultimate goal.

In this work, I have used the excellent translation of the Qur'an titled *The Qur'an: A Complete Revelation* by Sam Gerrans and give him credit for the many ideas and concepts in my work. I invite the interested reader to read his translation of the Qur'an at *reader.quranite.com*.

As a believer, it is my sacred duty to call people to God and I have written this book solely for this purpose. It is my ardent hope that the sincere student will do his own due diligence on the Qur'an and, if God wills, be gifted with an unshakable faith in God alone so he can truly serve the Lord of all creation.

Introduction to Tyranny 2.0

We are living under a tyranny disguised as a democracy. The genius of its architects is that they have camouflaged it in the doublespeak of choice, freedom and democracy; but make no mistake, we face a tyranny unparalleled by any of its predecessors in its scale and sophistication. Whereas, the tyrannies of old employed crude methods of torture and mass slaughter to subjugate the masses; Tyranny 2.0 employs the refined scientific method. It applies knowledge gained from the disciplines of biology, chemistry, computer science, mathematics, physics and psychology in its management of the human herd; continuously learning, refining its algorithms and perfecting its methods in order to achieve its ultimate goal of complete control over the human mind.

The fake pandemic of 2020 kicked off the global implementation of totalitarian lockdowns, mandatory face masks and forced injections. This is but a taste of the dystopian future that awaits us if we do not repent, reform and warn. It may sound cliché, but time *is* running out. Tyranny 2.0 is now officially online and our technocratic overlords have made it clear that they mean business.

Yet, even now, most men are unaware (or in denial) that we are living under a tyranny. The truth is that "God guides whom He wills".[236] It is not within my power to *wake* you up, nor can I convince a victim of brainwashing that he, in fact, *is* brainwashed. This book is only for those who understand that we are in the grips of a sophisticated tyranny, and believe in God; for it is God alone who can save us.

The harsh reality is that we are ruled by corrupt, sinful and evil men. It makes no difference whether they call themselves Christians, Jews, Muslims or atheists, nor does it matter whether they are the leaders of the "free world", third-world dictators, directors of intelligence agencies or the Pharaohs of Egypt, these men are workers of corruption and have no qualms about ordering the slaughter of millions to get what they want.

---

[236] *The Qur'an*, 28:56.

Contrary to popular propaganda, the rulers of our current tyranny are not the champions of the people, but are their very enemies. This is to be expected since the corrupt selection process of Tyranny 2.0 ensures that only the most vile and devious of the lot rise to the top of the power structure.

These evildoers – and their predecessors – have been waging a secret war against mankind for the better part of a century. Their aim is to destroy man's dignity, decency and morality. Ultimately, they wish to extinguish our very soul.

Tyranny 2.0 uses cutting edge *soft* weapons against its principal enemy: men. It uses cellphones, email and social media to track, monitor and surveil us. It leverages the internet and television to deliver devastating payloads of propaganda, pornography and entertainment to keep us docile and apathetic. It markets pharmaceutical weapons of pills, injections and packaged foods to deliver hormone altering chemicals, gene editing instructions and GMO foods to destroy our health. It funds social movements to promote homosexuality, women liberation and racial equality to pervert our culture. When all else fails, it deploys drones, smart bombs and mercenaries to kill, slaughter and torture, to obliterate entire nations.

Any reasonable thinking man can now work out that the motive behind such monstrous acts is not "to champion liberty and democracy"[237] across the world. We have been conditioned to accept such outright lies by those in power because this entire system is based on deception.

Tyrants wage war in order to control systems, resources, and people. They know that they must control all resources in order to guarantee their position as the apex predator. However, our enlightened tyrants have come to understand that if they wish to rule forever, they must ultimately control the human mind; and they are tantalizingly close to this goal.

---

237 Biden, Joseph R., and Jr. "Why America Must Lead Again." Foreign Affairs, Council on Foreign Relations, 30 Nov. 2020, www.foreignaffairs.com/articles/united-states/2020-01-23/why-america-must-lead-again.

The first rule of any conflict is to know your enemy. All evidence points to the United States – considering its superpower status – as the primary cultural, economic and environmental corrupter in the land, but that is seeing the trees for the forest. The people of the United States – and the Western civilization – have, themselves, been under a continuous assault by a sinister force for the better part of a century. It was only after this force of evil had compromised the religion, culture and family values of the West that it set its sights upon the rest of the world.

What is this sinister force and why is it hell bent on destroying humanity? You may already have a hazy idea of its nature even though modern propaganda has done all that it can to convince you of its non-existence. I am, of course, talking about Satan, the Deceiver. Tyranny 2.0 is based entirely on deception precisely because it is a Satanic tyranny and, as we shall see, deception is *the* modus operandi of Satan.

God in His final revelation to mankind, the Qur'an, warns us of this malevolent being whose objective is nothing short of our utter humiliation and destruction. The seriousness of God's warning cannot be overstated. He exhorts us to take Satan as a clear enemy and exercise our utmost vigilance against his attempts to divert us from the righteous path of God. Satan wishes to enslave us in this world and lead us to Hell in the next; and he achieves this by partnering with tyrants, old and new.

The Qur'an details the account of an ancient tyrant, Pharaoh, who was also in the thrall of Satan. His tyranny used religion, sorcery and finance to subjugate its population; not unlike Tyranny 2.0 which uses science, the entertainment industry and banks to subjugate us. Pharaoh's tyranny committed genocide by slaughtering a certain faction of the population; not unlike Tyranny 2.0 which commits global genocide – the depopulation agenda – by the scientific means of feeding the populace processed GMO foods and pesticide tainted crops, facilitating abortion and, more recently, COVID-19 "vaccines". Pharaoh sought to discover the God of Moses and the means of the heavens; not unlike Tyranny 2.0 which is launching sophisticated telescopes and satellites to peer into the heavens, and constructing state-of-the-art particle accelerators to study the building blocks of the universe.

But, perhaps, the most striking of all connections between Pharaoh's tyranny and Tyranny 2.0 is their use of obelisks to mark their domain. These obelisks are now erected in most of the cities around the world. The most famous of them, the Washington Monument, is a popular tourist attraction in Washington D.C. Every President of the United States faces this obelisk during his swearing in ceremony, promising to protect and defend Tyranny 2.0.

Satan uses the elites of Tyranny 2.0 to implement his agenda of enslaving mankind; and they are rewarded well for their services. However, theirs is a losing deal because on the Day of Judgment, Satan and his followers will enter Hell and remain there forever; an evil end for evil works. If that was the end of the matter, I would not be writing this book. But, unfortunately, it is not.

The people – by informed consent and active participation in this Satanic system – are guilty as well. They worship the idols of Tyranny 2.0 instead of worshipping God. They turn to the idols of state, religion and medicine to seek safety, guidance and health, when they should be seeking these blessings from God. They worship themselves when they should be worshipping God. They fear men when they should be fearing God. These tendencies are termed as *making partners with God* within the theology of the Qur'an, the only unforgivable sin.[238] If the people do not repent and reform, they will enter Hell along with their leaders.

This is a spiritual war and at stake is our very soul. The pain, suffering and humiliation that we experience in this life is but a shadow of the eternal pain and suffering that awaits the apathetic, amoral, and appetite driven souls in Hell.

The Qur'an calls those who believe in God and the life to come to work on disciplining and purifying themselves. They must stop consuming

---
238 The Qur'an 4:48.

the filth churned out by Tyranny 2.0 and struggle to escape, as much as possible, from its grip. God promises His help, provision and refuge to those who resist Satan and assures them a place in the eternal Garden in the Hereafter. We must warn men of the impending judgment of God which will can only be averted from those who fear God and take the Almighty as their sole Ally and Protector.

***

Many of the ideas presented in this book are from the ground-breaking work of Sam Gerrans titled *The Qur'an: A Complete Revelation*. I encourage you to download his work – which is available for free[239] – and go through it carefully.

I would be remiss if I did not mention the impact Alan Watt's talks[240] – have had on my world-view. His piercing insights into the inner workings of this Satanic system and the staggering scale of its deception have influenced many of my own ideas in this work.

All translations, unless otherwise noted, are my own. I have striven to render the Arabic in a literal, direct and consistent manner, being particularly influenced by the unique styles of John J. Arberry, Sahih International and Sam Gerrans. Where a literal translation of a phrase was too confusing, I have opted for a somewhat looser rendering, but have footnoted the literal translation for the interested reader.

Introduction to Cosmology of the Qur'an

In this work, I present the cosmology and astronomy of the Qur'an. Try as you might, you cannot escape the fact that what the Qur'an presents a model of celestial and terrestrial phenomena is utterly irreconcilable with science and the claims of its priesthood – the scientific class. Scientists would have us believe that the universe is an ever expanding, never ending space without any physical boundaries. In this space, countless objects spin, collide and orbit. Utter chaos reigns supreme. The earth is relegated to the status of just another planet among countless others

---

239 https://quranite.com
240 http://cuttingthroughthematrix.com

in this limitless universe. The sun is at the center of our solar system around which all planets – including the earth – revolve.

However, this is not what the Qur'an presents as fact.

The Qur'an repeatedly refers to the sky as a raised physical structure and the ground as a plane. It speaks of seven skies stacked on top of each other. It states that the ground is firmly fixed by mountains and that it is sun and the moon that are in motion, not the ground. However, the lamentable state of affairs is such that Muslims – who vehemently proclaim the Qur'an to be right and true – are unwilling to challenge the false claims presented by science. Even a cursory understanding of the word of God lays bare the lies present in the heliocentric model – to speak nothing of a myriad of other falsehoods peddled by Darwin, Newton and Einstein. If you are uncomfortable with this statement, then I suggest you ponder on what your eyes bear witness to every day: the sun has been travelling across the sky your whole life! You have been blinded by deceivers who would rather you shut out your eyes to the truth. Only a man conditioned by years of propaganda, disinformation and lies[10] rejects the testimony of his eyes and claims that it is not the sun that is moving but the very ground itself!

In this work, I will go over the treatment of the words samā and arḍ – and auxiliaries – in the Qur'an. Below are two verses containing these words so we are clear on what is being discussed:

> He who appointed the *arḍ* a floor and the *samā* a construction and sent down from the *samā* water so He brought forth fruits from it for your provision. So do not appoint equals to God when you know.
> (2:22)

> Or like a cloudburst from *samā* – in it is darkness, thunder and lightning – they put their fingers in their ears against the thunder fearing death. And God encompasses the unbelievers
> (2:19)

The Qur'an uses the word *arḍ* to denote the ground on which we stand. This word is usually translated as: earth, world or land. I like the rendering of *arḍ* as ground since this word does not come with baggage. What I mean by that is that words such as earth and world have been associated with a false spinning globe for so long that it is impossible to get the reader to visualize anything different when reading them. *Arḍ* is defined in Arabic dictionaries as: earth (as apposed to heaven or as a planet), globe, world, soil, ground, country and land. The Qur'an uses the word *samā* to denote the sky. This word is usually translated as: sky, heaven or firmament. I keep it simple by rendering it as sky throughout my work. *Samā* is defined in Arabic dictionaries as: to be high, elevated, raised, erect, lofty, tall, eminent and prominent.

We will investigate various verses in the Qur'an to build a true understanding of the phenomena around us. No trickery or falsehood is employed – personally, I am sick of both. A word on translation: It is understood that all translators have some bias; man is incapable of being truly impartial, try as he may. I am no exception. I have tried my best to render my translation in a direct, literal and consistent manner. I have also consulted a large number of translations and other works in my rendering of Qur'anic verses, a full list of which can be found in the References section. I sincerely advise you to ponder on the information below and not dismiss out of hand that which challenges your knowledge and assumptions. A book claiming to be from God deserves sincere, measured and careful study. May God guide you to His straight path.

Let us begin, then, **in the name of God.**

REFERENCE

Books
The Qur'an: A Complete Revelation, Sam Gerrans. *quranite.com*

Online Resources
reader.quranite.com

Website
willyounotreason.com

Email
contact@willyounotreason.com

www.ingramcontent.com/pod-product-compliance
Lightning Source LLC
Chambersburg PA
CBHW072212070526
44585CB00015B/1307